Contents of Accompanying DVD

INTRODUCTION
VIDEO PERFORMANCES

1) "Oh quante volte," from I CAPULETI ED I MONTECCHI by Bellini
   Giulietta: Kristi Trimble, soprano

2) "Sul fil d'un soffio etesio," from FALSTAFF by Verdi
   Nannetta: Elizabeth Wiles, soprano

3) "The Piano Song," by Irving Berlin
   Elizabeth King, soprano, assisted by Stephen Dubberly

4) "Fra poco a me ricovero," from LUCIA DI LAMMERMOOR by Donizetti
   Edgardo: Ken Goodenberger, tenor

5) "E lucevan le stelle," from TOSCA by Puccini
   Cavaradossi: Ralph Sanders (Rafael Sanderi), tenor

6) "Scena del velo," from DON CARLO by Verdi
   Eboli: Andrea Jaber, mezzo-soprano
   Tebaldo: Katherine McDaniel, soprano

7) "Largo al factotum," from IL BARBIERE DI SIVIGLIA by Rossini
   Il Barbiere: Richard Rovin, baritone

8) "La Calunnia," from IL BARBIERE DI SIVIGLIA by Rossini
   Don Basilio: Orival Bento-Gonçalves, bass

9) "Old Man River," from SHOWBOAT by Jerome Kern
   Leon Turner, bass

AUDIO PERFORMANCES

1) "Je dis que rien ne m'épouvante," from CARMEN by Bizet
   Micaëla: Barbara Divis, soprano

2) "La Madre al figlio lontano," song by I. Pizzetti
   Layna Chianakas, mezzo-soprano

3) "Una furtiva lagrima," from L'ELISIR D'AMORE by Donizetti
   Nemorino: Thomas Truhitte, tenor

4) "Ah, lêve-toi, soleil!" from ROMÉO ET JULIETTE by Gounod
   Roméo: Michele Sommese, tenor

5) "Di provenza il mar il sol," from LA TRAVIATA by Verdi
   Germont: Richard Rovin, baritone

6) "Danse Macabre," song by C. Saint-Saens
   Orival Bento-Gonçalves, bass

AUTHOR BIOGRAPHY AND PHOTO ALBUM

Notes on the DVD:

1. Menus remain for 1 minute and then revert to source menu. At the main menu, a random play of the 9 video performances will begin after 1 minute of inaction.

2. All playback controls (PLAY, PAUSE, FAST FWD/REV, 1-MIN. SKIPS [FWD & REV]) are available in the general and soprano, mezzo-soprano, and tenor vocalises. Due to disk space limits, baritone and bass have only PLAY, PAUSE, and 1-MIN. SKIPS (FWD & REV).

Vocal Rescue

Vocal Rescue

Rediscover the Beauty, Power, and Freedom in Your Singing

by
Lois Alba

William Andrew
publishing

ISBN: 0-8155-1506-5

Published in the United States by
William Andrew Publishing
13 Eaton Avenue
Norwich, NY 13815

Cover and interior design by Brent Beckley
Photo of Michael Jones as Timur in TURANDOT (Anchorage Opera) by Jim Lavrakas; all other photos from the author's private collection.

Manufactured in the United States of America

Printed on acid-free paper

10 9 8 7 6 5 4 3 2 1

Library of Congress Cataloging-in-Publication Data

Alba, Lois.
   Vocal Rescue: rediscover the beauty, power and freedom in your
singing / by Lois Alba
      p. cm.
   Includes bibliographical references and index.
   ISBN 0-8155-1506-5
1. Singing--Instruction and study. I. Title

MT820.A42 2004
783--dc22
                          2004009917

Dedication

This book is dedicated to a great singer-teacher, Elena Nikolaidi. It was my good fortune to be associated with her for 25 years before her passing in 2002 at the age of 96. It is rare that a great singer is also a great teacher, but "Nicky" was both.

From her earliest successes at the Staatsoper in Vienna, under the guidance of Bruno Walter, to her brilliant debut as a recitalist in New York followed by contracts to sing in all of the great opera houses throughout the world, she was a unique and dynamic performer. She was equally at home in recital literature. The intimacy of the lied was, for her, a means of true communication, as it was for her predecessor, Lotte Lehmann.

For me, Nicky's greatest gift was her intuitive sense about teaching. She loved to inspire her students to join her in her excitement of the sheer joy of singing. Even in her last years, she could indicate in a few notes the direction the student must take. Nicky loved to talk about the art of singing...its simplicity, spontaneity, and the need to "just do it." She inspired me to teach and was always encouraging me to continue.

When my pupils had successes, she was quick to praise us. She is in every part of this book. Fortunately, I have saved many tapes of lessons with her and a marvelous talk about her life which we recorded a few years ago in Tallahassee. It was the occasion of a celebration of her years at Florida State University, which included a concert of a group of her star singers. Carlisle Floyd had brought her there to teach many years before. Mme. Nicky "took" the stage that night, like the true diva she was, as she thanked all her friends and colleagues. The poem "Why I Teach" grew out of the inspiration I received from working with her. Thank you, Nicky.

Why I Teach

To teach is to share the gifts that have come through our teachers…

Those inspired muses who love giving of themselves.

It is their mission to pass on their discoveries,

Their knowledge and their songs not sung.

To teach is to take part in a metamorphosis,

To see the light come into faces who have forgotten why they sing…

Who have lost the joy of music for itself.

To teach is to coax forth the kernel of truth in each singer…

To lead them to find their unique sound.

To allow discussion, to invite inquiry.

To simplify, demystify.

To celebrate the coming of the truth for each…

Their own uniqueness.

Only then music is free to be born and shared again.

Lois Alba

Contents

Lois Alba as Fiordiligi in COSÌ FAN TUTTE
at Teatro Bellini, Catania, Sicily

About the Author

I was born in Houston, Texas, and at the early age of eleven I heard my first opera. Then and there I decided that opera was to be my life. After performing in many opera houses throughout Europe, I became fascinated with the art of singing for itself. This led me to teaching, which I have done for twenty years. I recall that when I was just seventeen I received a letter from Kirsten Flagstad. After a concert, I had written her my one and only fan letter. Of course, I told her that I wanted to be a singer. Her final words in the letter were, "You must realize that a career in singing involves a lifetime of study." And so it is, but I find teaching as exciting and rewarding as singing. I never tire of hearing new voices and finding ways of simplifying the approach to singing with more spontaneity and ease.

After returning from Italy I lived in New York for some years, during which time I formed a small company named Opera Rediviva, with Richard Kapp as conductor. With his orchestra, the Philharmonia Virtuosi, we produced rare operatic masterpieces, including Pacini's SAFFO and Rameau's LES BORÉADES in Town Hall. When I later moved to Houston I continued to sponsor concerts with a group I formed, which led to the founding of Opera in the Heights, a small company. I was artistic director there for the first two years after which I elected to resign. A year later I created The Black Tie Opera Ensemble, to give performances of operatic excerpts. These were all successful ventures, but they left me less time to concentrate on my teaching and writing.

After much encouragement from my students, I began to write about the art of singing. My first book, *Studio to Stage*, brought me many aspiring singers who continue to coach with me while following their own successful careers.

My desire in writing this book is to demystify the technical aspects of singing and thus to free the singer to his or her highest sense of creativity and spontaneity. My eleven years of study in Italy, where bel canto, or beautiful singing, originated in the seventeenth century, as well as my nine years in the opera there, have given me many insights into the art.

I have my studio in Houston where I reside with my husband.

Preface

The challenges to arrive at a successful career in singing, and particularly in opera, seem almost impossible to many singers because of technical problems, a fear of high notes, lack of projection and, most importantly, confusion as to how to express music unhampered by technical preoccupation. As a performer and now a teacher, I am aware of all the pitfalls. This has inspired me to organize and synthesize the techniques I have acquired after many years of study.

My own search for the truths about singing have spanned many years, beginning at age twelve when I began to study. My first teacher had been a pupil of the famous contralto, Ernestine Schumann-Heink. Her explanations were simple and I was not bombarded with all the technical terms I later heard. I had a sense of ease with the few exercises she taught me. The seventeenth and eighteenth century Italian songs and a few German lieder were my studies. I also heard many great singers in those early years. There were concert recital series that brought all the "stars" to Houston. Among them were Ezio Pinza, Marian Anderson, Jussi Bjöerling, Dorothy Maynor, and Roland Hayes. I was filled with high hopes for a career in singing.

Soon after graduating from high school at age sixteen, I went to New York, and it was while attending a very well known music school there that

I began having my first doubts about my voice. High notes became more and more difficult and I lost my nerve about performing. My first teacher heard me the following summer and was appalled at my effortful singing. My voice had grown thick and unwieldy and there was a noticeable change of "registers" that I had learned to observe.

On my return to New York I found a teacher outside the school. Mario Pagano was a Neapolitan who had sung in Italy as a tenor until a tonsillectomy ruined his voice. He was a simple, unassuming man who understood sound and based his teaching on his ear and his intuition. From him, I began to understand the true meaning of bel canto. He was also responsible for my decision to study in Italy one day.

In my early twenties, I had the opportunity to study with Rosa Ponselle. She had been my idol since I had first heard her voice on the old 78 rpm records purchased in one of the many stores on New York's 6th Avenue. There I also bought records of singers such as Caruso, Tito Schipa, Gigli, and Eva Turner. The memory of hearing Ponselle sing in her magnificent living room at "Villa Pace" is as vivid today as that first lesson with her.

Ponselle's approach was simple, based on the use of the breath. The sounds she made were rich as well as an example of a perfect legato. I use one particular exercise of hers to this day. You will find it in the Vocalise section. Hearing her and having those precious lessons convinced me even more that it is the ear that must be trained to recognize and identify the beauty of the sound. I also believe that each voice has its own unique quality and the ear can be trained to bring it forth. This further persuaded me that the real art of singing is not based on a list of muscles and their functions, or charts on anatomy.

Ponselle told me about her singing with Caruso and his affectionate nickname for her: "Caruso in gonnella," meaning "Caruso in a skirt." Their

Neapolitan heritage certainly gave them a similar color and sound. Two signed photographs, one in her library, and the other, a costume picture of her as Carmen, are among my cherished mementos, and are included in the Voice Types section and also in the Photo Album pictures in the enclosed DVD.

Another great singer, the unique Lotte Lehmann, was the inspiration for my decision to go to Europe. She included me in performances of DER ROSENKAVALIER at the Music Academy of the West in Santa Barbara. I spent an enchanted summer studying the Marschallin in preparation for my opera debut with the Houston Opera the following season. Lehmann no longer sang, but her face and speaking voice expressed every nuance when she directed the young cast. Since she had sung all three parts in the opera, she could "become" each of the three characters at will. I'll never forget her ability to transform her body and posture depending on which of the three parts she was acting (silently) as we sang. I also learned to love lieder, which she taught us in classes in which the marvelous pianist, Gwendolyn Koldofsky, accompanied us.

Studying with performers is very different from working with a pedagogue, *per se.* Singers with experience on the stage have been there, and can sense many pitfalls that the stage reveals, that singing at a piano or in a room cannot. A mere indication of a vocal idea from a performer can clarify what statistics and words fail to do.

One of my teachers, Luisa Pallazzini, had sung in the same company with Claudia Muzio for years. They shared performances of LA TRAVIATA. Her insights about Violetta learned from Muzio were invaluable to me for that part.

The last great artist I studied with was Elena Nikolaidi. When I returned after years of singing in Europe, I moved back to Houston. "Nicky," as everyone lovingly called her, was more interested in working with younger singers and really only consented to hear me because of the urging of a mutual friend. I sang an aria from LA FORZA DEL DESTINO, after which she began to work with me. For several years she guided me and gave me all kinds of insights about singing and teaching. When she retired she worked only with career singers who studied with her in their formative years. She was unstinting in her search for the beauty and communicativeness in the art of singing. She relied on her ear and the indications she could give to students. No involved explanations or charts for this lady. "Just do it" was her motto. Her love and inspiration will always be with me.

The teaching in Italy is more empirical compared to the concepts of singing taught by the pedagogues of today. The training I received in Italy was from several singers who were famous at La Scala. One of my favorites was the baritone, Carlo Tagliabue, who in his late sixties still sang wonderfully. I was taught by those from the schools of Vanzo, Delle Sedie, and Marietta Brambilla. The conductors I worked with had studied with maestri such as Marinuzzi, Mugnone, Gui, and Serafin. I have included material from the Bellini singers, Lablache, and Rubini, as well as Delle Sedie and Marietta Brambilla in the Vocalise section. Included there is also another treasure of mine, the little known work of Clara Doria.

I have acquired a collection of rare material on bel canto, including some vocalises that stress the comparison of vowels (as sung) in French, Italian, German, and English. The timbre of the voice and its beauty depend on the perception (the ear) of the singer and the direction of the teacher in the formation of the vowels. Breathing, that maligned subject, concerning "support," along with phrasing, *legato*, florid singing, style, tradition, and singing *recitativi* are all part of this study.

In closing, I want to explain that there are only a few simple concepts to bel canto. The main factor depends on the ear of the teacher and his or her ability to train the ear of the singer. This is the singer's true guide. The refinement of the ear comes with the keen awareness that develops as the principles described in this book are followed. It is your journey to becoming aware of the innate beauty in your sound.

In this era of computers, this study can be likened to reprogramming the mind and body to a new format: one based on freeing you to communicate music and text through the sound of your voice. And, like all new programs, this requires patience, application, and a keen desire to explore greater means for developing the vocal instrument in order to free you to your highest vocal and artistic potential.

This book is not meant to be a substitute for a teacher to guide you, but merely an outline of the principles of beautiful singing, bel canto, which have been handed down since the 1700s.

This book will help you discover and clarify your own voice…to free it rather than to teach you a "technique" for its own sake. It is designed to help you rediscover your spontaneity and freedom, and the joy that comes with learning how to sing beautifully.

Included throughout the book are a variety of special instructions and exercises I use with my students to help them understand the principles I teach. These are indicated by boxed text and a bird, to help you to easily refer back to them.

I have also included the council of many great singers and teachers and their vocal studies. These are "check-points" to help you evaluate your progress and to plan your goals. With these in mind, enjoy the process and make every day one of new discoveries about yourself, your voice, and "why" you want to sing.

Acknowledgments

I would like to thank my best friend and husband, Arthur Wachter, for his insights, suggestions, criticism, and never-ending encouragement. His background as an art director enabled him to contribute to many aspects of the book.

My thanks also go to Robert Land, who contributed invaluable help with the production of the DVD and CD accompanying the book, as well as fine photo designs. He too, contributed much enthusiasm for the work. Above all, I am indebted to my wonderful editor, Valerie Haynes, whose keen sense enabled her to make the work more accessible. Her joy and excitement were always inspiring.

Special thanks go to William Andrew Publishing, who published the book. Other important contributors were my ever-faithful daughter, Shelley Townsend, who was able to help me with sending out all the material by computer, my daughter, Jeri Wachter, for her fine artistic talents, Brent Beckley and Jeanne Roussel for their artistic layout design, and Barbara Divis, who helped with coordinating and forwarding materials.

Lastly, the book would not have been possible without all my teachers and my many students who continue to inspire me. Thanks to all!

An Introduction to
Bel Canto

The main purpose of this book is to demystify the secrets to beautiful singing. I will do this by giving you the seven key principles I use in my teaching. They are an amalgamation of many precepts I have learned through my years of study with a remarkable group of teachers, and from a large library of rare treatises on the art which I have compiled. No one person has all the answers, but the concepts outlined herein are what I believe will free the beauty and power of your voice, and they come from the fine art of vocal mastery known as bel canto.

The consensus of most of my teachers has been that singing is a natural outpouring of sound based on a few key elements. Nevertheless, there are many schools of thought on how to arrive at the ideal manner of singing. In the 1800s the Maestri described the process, but in the final analysis they were subjective in their interpretation of how to obtain the beauty of the voice. The Italians have written about the art since the 1800s, but even the earliest books are vague in the exact science. This so-called science came about much later when the son of the tenor Manuel Garcia, a once famous singer and teacher, as well as the father of the fabled Maria Malibran and her sister Pauline Viardot, invented the laryngoscope. After this, the singing profession began to rely on its "eyes" rather than its "ears" for vocal guid-

Art, in a word,
is life.
M. J. Guyau

ance. Many people believe this contributed to the decline of the real school of singing.

From all accounts, there are numerous ways to approach the study of singing, but I have found that the best teaching involves an acute sense of sound, intuition, and imagery. My experience in studying with several renowned singers as well as some fine Italian maestri has made me an advocate of the principle that true mastery of the voice and true vocal beauty come from developing the ear. The teacher indicates a direction, but your own perceptions must come from hearing great singing and recognizing your best sounds; that is, the best notes in your voice, followed by a fine tuning to make the whole scale homogeneous. I don't believe that the scientific or medical approach to sound will ever lead the singer to his full potential.

Parts 1 and 2 of this book present the essence of voice training. It is what I teach, and what all good voice teachers impart to their students in one way or another. It is not an explanation of a technique *per se*, but a philosophy, a way to think and feel to bring your body and mind together harmoniously to produce beautiful sound.

This is one of the most helpful instructions in this regard. Rather than focusing on the so-called technique of singing, focus on finding the most beautiful and consistent sounds and an even scale.

Bel Canto

Bel canto is identified with the Italian school of singing. It grew out of the flowering of music in the baroque period (1600-1750). The term "bel canto" was never used at that time, but was coined later to denote the vocal qualities of the singers in the baroque period.

The first half of the sixteenth century was a time in which singers appeared in chapels, and their style bore no semblance to what would later develop as opera. The writings for voice consisted of exchanges of improvisation between the voices and instruments, and by the second half of the seventeenth century the melodies became more expansive.

Two of the earliest writers of opera were Jacopo Peri and Claudio Monteverdi. The texts were about deities and historical characters from Greek and Roman antiquity. They favored the *stile spianato*, meaning unadorned, not florid, passages. As the use of ornamented writing developed, the ecstasy and vocal virtuosity were given to the *castrato*. This was an emasculated male whose voice retained the high range of a boy soprano. They sang major roles of mythological and historical heroes. Two famous castrati of that period were Tosi and Mancini, both of whom wrote books on singing.

The sounds of the lyric tenor or baritone were thought to be too harsh for agility. Women played male parts, and the castrati often played women's parts. There was a sense of "wonder" and great faith in the expressive qualities of singing, vocal timbre without demanding realism.

The specific period of bel canto is a direct emanation of the baroque. The phrase bel canto has come to mean beautiful singing of any music, but the real bel canto style in its inception was one of wonder, various timbres, a variety of color, and virtuosic display.

This is the esthetics of the style. The real bel cantists were the composers who wrote the music. Some of the earliest manifestations of opera were the works of the Florentine *Camerata*, which included Peri and Giulio Caccini (himself a vocal teacher), who based their composing on words and the so-called "reciting in song." When opera moved on to the baroque structure of the Roman and Venetian schools, the composers advocated melody, arias, and set pieces. The ideals of Platonic and Greek tragedy took a back seat. The discovery of vocal and histrionic expression came to the fore.

Rossini, Donizetti, and Bellini are the most well known composers whose works call for the principles demanded of the early teachers of bel canto. Rossini's ideal, as reported from a conversation in 1858, had three requirements: "A naturally beautiful voice, even throughout its range, careful training that encouraged effortless delivery of highly florid music, and a mastery of style that could only be assimilated from listening to the best Italian exponents."[*]

Look and you will find it. What is unsought will go undetected.
Sophocles

These words of Edward J. Meyer sum up the principles: "Nature was the great teacher and not man. Man, when he bases his teaching upon his own ideas of voice is too artificial; hence, artificiality. Witness the many ridiculous things singers are (now) taught to do. With such, the effort is to make the voice, to *compel it*, instead of *allow it*. Nature teaches differently. By a study of Nature and Nature's laws, the voice is allowed to develop; is allowed or induced to reveal itself instead of being made, compelled, or forced."[†]

---

[*] A. Michotte, An Evening Chez Rossini, 1858; Opera XVIII 1967; R. Celletti; La Storia del Belcanto Fiesole, 1983.

[†] J. Edmund and G. Meyer, *Position and Action in Singing* (Boston: Schirmer, 1911).

Part 1

The Secrets to
Beautiful Singing
(Bel Canto)

Vincenzo Bellini
Master composer of bel canto operas
(1801 - 1835)

Breathing

Breath Support

Breath is the life of the sound. Thus, "breath support" is the first principle all singers need to understand. Many "methods" that are given for arriving at the "support" of the breath, however, are both confusing and cause great rigidity in the body.

In fact, "support" has become a subject of great controversy. It does not mean HOLD OUT, DRIVE OUT, or PUSH PIANOS, books, or other heavy objects. To support the breath means, simply, to be conscious of the inhalation in a gentle manner and *mentally* sustain the sound by consciously emitting the minimum without strong pressure. It can be likened to sighing out the air.

To understand how breath supports the tone, observe something a bit more solid than airy breath: Watch how water follows the path of least resistance. A stream flows over rocks and around curves and over waterfalls. What supports it? It is not forced out of some giant hose. Rather, the natural forces of gravity that result from the Earth turning regularly on its axis (much like natural breathing) cause it to flow. If a dam is erected, however, this flow is blocked.

The breath should never be held back.
Lilli Lehmann

Breath supports tone in much the same way—natural breathing allows tone to follow the path of least resistance—*IF it is not blocked* by tense breathing, rigid bodies, tight lips, exaggerated vowels, and other misguided, "death-defying" attempts at SUPPORT!

Rosa Ponselle told me she felt as if her voice were on a tray. This is another good image of the sensation of the tone being easily supported.

As the brilliant coloratura Luisa Tetrazzini observed, "Certain young singers take in an enormous breath, stiffening every muscle in order to hold the air, thus depriving their muscles of all elasticity... Too much in-breathing and too violent an effort in inhaling will not help the singer at all. The attack of the sound must come from the *appoggio*, or breath prop."[*] To simplify this concept, think of the breath issuing from the lungs supporting the tone; the feeling is of leaning on the breath. This is *appoggio*.

Herbert Caesari made a similar observation: "Mediocrity invariably employs a blind, uncontrolled, and uncompromising maximum breath pressure; quality singers use a perfectly controlled indispensable minimum."[†]

Mio Dio. If God has not taught you how to breathe, it is time you were buried.

Vincenzo Cirillo (1623 - 1667) from *Il Bel Canto,* by Vittorio Ricci

Posture

Posture is often said to be the cure-all for support, but this doesn't mean a military stance, that is, rigid chest, held high, and very often the knees are locked. The ideal stance is one that offers easy balance and the feeling that the feet, legs, and torso support the body, leaving the lungs and throat free to act.

[*] Luisa Tetrazzini - from *The Art of Singing,* by S. Fucito and B.J. Beyer (F.A. Stokes, 1922)

[†] Herbert Caesari, *The Voice of the Mind* (London: Robert Hall, Ltd., 1951).

Once you have the right posture, movement about the stage will be more natural also.

Here are two images that can be used as exercises in posture:

The first is from a wonderful teacher, Bettye Gardner, with whom I studied movement. In addition to being a fine teacher of singing, she had also been a dancer, having studied with José Limon. She used much imagery in her teaching and this was her main expression:

The singer or actor must have the feeling of "tearing down" or "moving through" space. The desire to move through space with a strong impetus gives the body a sense of directed energy. Posture improves immediately and yet there is no stiffness.

This is the second image I find helpful:

Imagine having a string attached to the chest and being pulled forward by it. It is very easy to identify singers who move with this sense of focus.

Ease of Breath

Singing is an activity of the whole body. The energy is generated through the inhalation of breath. It is the life of the tone. Any rigidity in the body or the throat inhibits the free flow of the air (energy) to its points of resonation. Resonation occurs not only through the throat, head, and chest, but throughout the entire body.

My first teacher had studied with the famous contralto, Ernestine Schumann-Heink. Her simple guide for breathing was "expand low." This simple demand has an immediate effect. You feel a gentle expansion at the waist and the lungs gently expand. There is a feeling of being poised to initiate singing.

How should one breathe? To quote both Luciano Pavarotti and the great baritone, Piero Cappuccilli, "Like a newborn baby." An oversimplification you say? Try this exercise in natural breathing and use it whenever you are having difficulty relaxing in your breathing:

Lie on the floor, flat on your back. Observe where and how you breathe in this position. Feel the easy intake of the air, and the expansion of the back and waist as the lungs fill. The air easily and fully fills the lungs without your deliberately sucking it in.

After breathing while lying down, observe the same simple ease while standing. If you exhale consciously and allow the lungs to refill easily in the inhalation, you will be breathing as the Italians teach. In doing this, you will observe the ribs expand, the diaphragm descend, without being pushed down, and your abdomen will protrude slightly. It is an easy feeling and you will be able to move freely. Your whole body will be balanced, and there will be no conscious "holding" of breath. Above all, DO NOT LOCK YOUR KNEES!

This is the natural way to breathe. In contrast, setting muscles, pushing out, and holding out the ribs with a conscious effort, all produce tension.

Adelina Patti was once asked by an interviewer to explain her use of the diaphragm. Her answer was, "What is it? I am not familiar with it!"

A simple image of the diaphragm is that of a bowl that is facing downward. As the air is inhaled, the diaphragm (bowl) descends and the waist is expanded and there is also a feeling of expansion in the lower part of the rib cage.

Adequate Breath

Related to ease of breath is adequate breath. Many singers fear losing their breath and complain of being unable to finish phrases. The truth is they are holding back the breath in tension, and not using up what they have. In turn, they inhale more breath and finally become too full of breath while stopping its flow at the same time! There is a feeling of the breath almost being trapped near the upper chest and throat. This is a sure sign that the singer is not allowing the breath to nourish the sound, and it is being held back and compressed. The feeling is of having no more breath. The contrary is true, but it cannot be freed up for the sound.

The Breath Initiates the Tone

In starting a sound, it is best to use minimal breath in the initiation of it. This avoids flooding the sound and making phrasing and dynamics impossible. Listen to Renée Fleming or watch her on TV. There is a poised, quiet start of the phrase. Even if the phrase is dramatic and *forte*, think of a slender approach—lighter, and then increase the energy immediately *without* attempting to make more space for the larger sound. The Italians say that every note is initiated lightly, and immediately reinforced.

Let's look at the initial breath the singer takes to initiate the tone. First, the throat should be absolutely quiet and the tongue must not "pre-prepare" while the inhalation takes place. A consequent reaction is that the nostrils open like the sensation felt when you are about to sneeze.

Don't confuse readiness with tension. It is expectancy with complete stillness. Observe the high diver before the dive. It is a moment of complete focus...like the serve of tennis champions, the golfer at the tee, the free-throw of the basketball "great," and the pulling of the bow in archery.

When the smallest stream of air sets the cords in motion and the tone is initiated, the support called for from the diaphragm will naturally assert it-self—*if it is not deliberately pushed by the singer*!

This must be done with clear, undivided attention to the vowel and pitch operating as one; do not "scoop" under the pitch. This is the first secret of spontaneous and expressive singing. It is not a muscular thrust. During inhalation there must be absolute stillness in the larynx and the tongue.

Try breathing through the nose with the mouth slightly open. This will ensure the stillness of the tongue. One common expression of the Italians is that the in-breath should feel like smelling a fragrant flower. This prepares the sound for the *appoggio*. It literally means leaning into the sound, or leaning on the breath.

An image that may be helpful for the continuity of the breath and sound is the image of a thread being drawn through a needle. The head of the needle does not enlarge as the sound becomes louder. If the sound is the thread as it is drawn through, the only change in the sound is the speed and intensity through which it is conceived without manipulating the throat to achieve it.

Do not confound the compression of air with the pressure (gentle) of air. The correct sensation is that of the slight pressure on the accel-erator in a car. It is smooth, not a harsh movement. If the air is not allowed to flow, the result is rigid and then driven.

Look to the quality of your tone for economy of breath *instead* of your breathing muscles.

If you listen from the outside, it is like stopping to hear if the train is coming. It produces the holding of the breath. From the first note of the introduction of your music, "tune in" to the rhythm of the piece. Your breathing should be in "sync" with it so that your first note seems to be a continuation of the preceding music.

Droning the sound gives a feeling of continuity in the use of the breath. This does not mean slurring under the pitches, but it is like saying the word "Hummmmmmmmm" and continuing it. Scales become perfectly clear when this concept is understood. Try this exercise:

> *Inhale easily and on a low pitch, and intone a note with a "V" before it, singing "VVVVVV." Notice that the stream of air is slight and the low pitch puts no strain on you. Notice how long the breath lasts.*

This exercise will prove to you that the vocal cords are activated by the breath; they act as a valve much as the "V" did. In contrast to this, any forcing or "jamming" a large amount of breath will force the tiny cords to be blown apart.

Breathe When You Breathe and Sing When You Sing

The extraordinary tenor Beniamino Gigli, a model of bel canto singing, once said, "When I breathe, I take in air, and when I sing, I only think of singing."

It is true that the mind cannot focus on two separate ideas and not be divided in attention. Hence, breathe when you breathe and sing when you sing. If you are holding on to the breath, and controlling the airflow with a conscious, measured effort, you are probably manipulating the throat to hold back the air, and your diaphragm cannot act naturally to help. The air feels "stuck," there is no flow, and you feel deprived of the necessary breath for the phrase.

If you can conceive of the vocal cords acting as a valve to the outgoing stream of air as it reaches them, you will not be tempted to force out the air, but will let the chords close as they must to initiate the sound. The word here is "let," not "force."

In conclusion, I want to sum up the subject of breathing with a few important points.

Any attempt to deliberately and consciously work the diaphragm in expansion and contraction is not employing the free flow of air from the lungs. They must refill themselves in proportion as the breath is exhausted, by their own law—that is, action and reaction—not by consciously regulating the movement of the diaphragm. Failure to observe this principle leads to a mechanical, forced production of tone. This is why I often ask singers to deliberately exhale and to observe how the lungs immediately refill. It is the tone that regulates the expenditure of the air and the tone is controlled mentally by the demand of the singer's ear and sense of beauty. The exercise of observing the relaxation and freedom in the intake of air is explained earlier in this chapter.

If the music calls for a rigorous utterance, the singer, through his emotion, will demand this and call forth more energy. If the sound required is softer and gentler, the imagery of the singer will call forth more delicacy in the initiation of the sound and the breath will be expended more slowly. The diaphragm is brought into play only in the act of emitting the sound itself. It acts through, or as a result of, the demand for tone—not by being initiated directly beforehand. The demand for inhalation causes the diaphragm to react to its inflow of air. The air does not enter because of the preemptive movement of the diaphragm. It is a reaction, not a separate movement!

These observations are not ordinarily pointed out, and it is possible to become skillful in consciously regulating the breath with diaphragmatic control, but to my mind, it is at the expense of spontaneity, freedom, and the emotional content of the voice.

Of course, the ideal is the ability to inhale while maintaining the body without tension. Here is an exercise to gauge how much tension you have in the body while inhaling:

Close your mouth and draw in a deep breath through your nostrils. You will feel the lungs inflate and the whole body will seem to expand ever so gently. Now close your nostrils with your thumb and forefinger so that no breath can escape, and while observing this for ten seconds or so.... loosen and relax your whole body as much as possible without letting go of the breath. Then open your mouth and sigh out easily.

When you repeat this exercise, you will be able to ascertain how much unnecessary tension there is in your breathing.

A final thought: The more you rely on the simplest means for breathing and the gentle release of all the tension you feel in your body, the more singing will finally become an involuntary act, subject only to your desire to express yourself through the music.

Resonance

"When the soul wishes to experience something, she throws an image of the experience out before her and enters into her own image."

This is one of my favorite quotes, from an unknown person, and it describes beautifully how the singer can free the voice. It is also a wonderful metaphor for how a singer resonates.

What Is Resonance?

The word "resonance" comes from the Italian word *risonare*, meaning to re-sound. Its characteristic is akin to a hum. If you say the "hum" and then sing it, you will feel the vibrations in your face, throat, or chest, depending on the pitch you choose. It is a simple experiment showing us that there are areas that amplify the sound. It demonstrates how different parts of the body resonate with different pitches and with different types of focus.

How and Where Does the Voice Resonate?

The carrying power of the voice is not limited to the vocal cords. The vocal chords are not the producers of resonance *per se*. They are the transmitters through which the air must pass before resonation takes place. The most commonly accepted areas of resonation are the hard palate, the pharynx, and the frontal sinuses. However, the whole body resonates to varying degrees, depending on the pitch and quality of the tone. In particular, there are sensations in the larynx, the pharynx, the mouth, the nasal passages, and the chest, which amplify what would be a very limited sound without these vibrators.

These areas of resonation are activated as a result of the action of the vocal chords. (We say they are reflectors.) And it is the *ear* which is the regulator. (We will get more into that in subsequent chapters.)

It is not my purpose to set hard and fast rules for directing the thought to the areas of resonation while singing. The pitch, the area of the voice range on any note, calls the proper resonation into action.

Every artist was first an amateur.
Ralph Waldo Emerson

I believe that in any note there must be "something" relative to the whole range of the voice. For instance, in a low note where the chest resonance is more active, there must still be resonance from a higher octave; this gives what I call a homogeneous relationship to the entire scale.

Blocks to Resonation

The piano keyboard removed from the piano case is without sound. The piano needs the case for resonation. Likewise, the vocal chords use the whole body as a means of resonation.

On the other hand, if when we sing we deny the other parts of the body—the chest and the whole frame—we literally rely only on the head or the "mask," and sing from the *neck up*.

For example, to try to direct the air, to manipulate the throat for greater resonance and power, to physically attempt to "open the throat" and keep the larynx low are all tricks that interfere with the natural sound, and with resonance.

As stated in the chapter on Breathing, singing is an activity of the *whole body*. The *energy* is generated by inhaling and expelling the breath, and is the *life* of the tone. Any rigidity in the body or throat will inhibit this free flow of air (energy) to its points of resonation. These points of resonation, to where the energy/air must freely flow, are in the throat, head and chest, and throughout the entire body.

The Ear Regulates the Tone

Lilli Lehmann once said, "Learning and teaching to hear is the first task of both pupil and teacher… It is the only way to perfection."* As this suggests, the ear is the regulator of the voice, and the demand for sound is the solution to voice freedom. The spontaneity and freedom of the voice depend on a crystal clear idea of what pitch, what vowel, and what tempo the music calls for. The ear is the guide to the above action. It is not a "method" formula.

Many beautiful voices have been ruined by the study of technique, which makes the "method" the principle concern, and the ear is no longer the guide for the singer.

To describe how these approaches differ, let's use a metaphor comparing the difference between the computer and the artist. The computer has brought forth remarkable technical advances to speed up work, to compute vast amounts of data, to organize, and to print. Realizing its efficiency depends on the user, whose goal is to make the machine do work in the fastest way to perform multiple tasks that would take a human days, months, or even years. The human heart is not involved in the operation. It is a task of logic.

For the artist, the complete opposite is true. It is the human element that is engaged, and rushing it or compartmentalizing it will only de-

Resonance is an effect, not a cause. It is an element of reenforcement to the voice.
Clara Doria – *The Philosophy of Singing*

* Lilli Lehmann, *How to Sing* (New York: The MacMillan Co., 1914)

stroy any vestiges of beauty. Thus with singing, the singer's real goal should be the *freeing* of the voice to allow his heart, feelings, and expression to be heard. If the singer attempts physically to control the tongue as if it were some type of computer keyboard, this surely will impede its natural reaction. This will further prevent the natural impetus from the diaphragm, which cannot take place if the tone is controlled by the tongue.

The old Italian technique of teaching was empirical. Very little was written about resonance, and the teacher, through example, indicated what he wanted from the student—always emphasizing the importance of the ear as the guide for perfecting the voice.

In contrast, some of the most common expressions given to young singers today are to "direct the voice into the mask," "place the voice in the head," "sing forward," "open the throat," "raise the soft palate," or "make a furrow with your tongue." All of these statements are attempts to *control* the voice to produce sound. These may be the *effects* and *results* of singing well, but these physically controlled acts will not allow the singer to achieve vocal freedom. As I state elsewhere, rigidity in any form is the enemy of resonance!

Acquiring the Ideal Resonance

Consider a great actor on stage performing a powerful role. His voice fills the theatre and as he bellows, the chandeliers vibrate and the audience shivers. The power of the actor's voice is controlled by his intensity in speaking the text. He projects his *energy*. This intensity and energy are a function of his emotional motivation.

Similarly, with the singer, the motivation to sing and express the music brings the energy to focus on the sound intended.

Although there are no hard and fast rules for acquiring resonance, it is

The sound must be attacked in a frank and precise manner without preparing it and without arriving by sliding into the sound.

Trans. from
MÉTHODE de Parigi

dependent on the *ear*, on *imagery*, and on *intuition*. It is these that will bring the emotional motivation into focus.

For the beginning student, acquiring resonation can also mean *imitation*. The student needs to explore, through different vowels and combinations of them, mentally conceived, the ideal resonance. This study requires a persistent effort to feel and hear the *center* of the sound. The image can be likened to a pebble thrown into a pool of water. From the place where it enters the water there are concentric circles. This is similar to the overtones in resonance.

The clearer your intention as to the pitch, vowel, word, and emotion, the more resonant the sound will become. However, attention to excessive support or attempting to consciously direct sounds to the resonating cavities will result in bodily tension. It will also hold back the breath, impeding its free flow, and consequently, impede the resonance.

Humming can help you become conscious of vibrations in the head and chest, especially if the jaws are not closed. Try this exercise:

Learning and teaching to hear is the first task of both pupil and teacher...It is the only way to perfection.
Lilli Lehmann –
How to Sing

A discovery is said to be an accident meeting a prepared mind.
Albert Szent-Gyorgyi

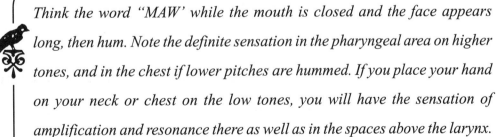

Think the word "MAW" while the mouth is closed and the face appears long, then hum. Note the definite sensation in the pharyngeal area on higher tones, and in the chest if lower pitches are hummed. If you place your hand on your neck or chest on the low tones, you will have the sensation of amplification and resonance there as well as in the spaces above the larynx.

Sound travels in two directions. The air in the cavities vibrates below the vocal chords as much as it vibrates above the vocal chords. This is an image I find very helpful to my students:

Imagine the lower note being in a higher place and the upper note being in a lower place. This helps achieve an evenness in the scale, arpeggio, *or ascending phrase. This image, in fact, is the exact truth about what takes place in the throat. For low pitches the larynx rises slightly (not with the singer's help), and the larynx lowers for higher pitches.*

Vowels and Timbre and Their Effect on Resonance

In a later chapter I explain vowels and timbre more completely, but I do want to mention here their effect on resonance.

There are no hard and fast rules for what vowel is the most favorable one for a singer to practice. The teacher must determine which is ideal for each voice. But here are some examples of how adjusting the timbre can affect the resonance, making the sound more full of life:

If a voice is overly dark and wobbly, often the singer pronounces "a" as "ah." To adjust this, try using a sound like the "a" in the word "sad" or "apple" to direct the sound to more life.

If the singer's sound is too bright, the vowel "ah" (often pronounced in this case like the word "mama" as said by a baby) can be rounded to sound more like the word "pause."

A vowel which is very often spoken too narrowly is the "eh" in a word like "same." It is frequently a diphthong and limits the flow of the sound. I stress the more open sound of "eh" in its pure form.

A too bright "ee" vowel is helped by pronouncing a "gn" sound, as in "gnye," or by thinking the word "wheat," pronouncing the "h." The section on vowel modification as it applies to range will clarify this concept more fully.

Once the singer is able to distinguish the feeling of freedom and the different timbre that these vowels can add to the sound, the mere thought of them will give all vowels and sounds more color and resonance.

In Conclusion

If a singer begins to feel "shut down" or his voice is diminishing in size and color, it is time to question his technique. The more the sound is felt to be coming into or toward the singer, not forced out to "project," the more it will gain in resonance, not "drive."

Resonance is the effect of "allowing" the sound to seek its own vibrating surface. The singer must be aware of the energy of vibratory sensation in all parts of the body. The whole body must be conceived of as a part of the sound itself. It is a "tuning fork," if you will. It must remain pliable and balanced to move in any direction—not dependent on a static manner of singing, which inhibits its free movement.

The range of the voice determines where the vibration is felt. The lowest pitches, which feel close to the chest, have a kind of rumble in the feel of the sound. The middle voice is sensed more in the mouth and nose area, while the resonance in highest pitches is felt less and seems to be in a narrow place. I again stress that these are *effects* and not suggestions to "direct" the sound to the areas mentioned.

If the emission of a note is easy and the metal (center) of the voice is noble, it means the singer has found the right position of the mouth.

Trans. A. Bach – from *Il Bel Canto*, by Vittorio Ricci

Registers

While the principles of singing are identical for all voices, each singer will ultimately create a unique effect by virtue of the quality of his or her voice. To use Caruso's metaphor, the quality of the voice depends on the singer's genetics (the marble) and artistry—"the hand, the heart, and the intellect." But in addition to this, each voice will differ in quality within its own range, as it moves up and down the scale.

Explaining Registers and Passaggi

Basing my work on sensations and the ear, not physiology, I prefer to say that there are low, medium, and high areas, or so-called registers, of the voice. There are many theories about where these divisions occur in each voice of the same type. No voice is exactly like another in its mechanism. Nevertheless, the singer, when relaxed, is able to determine the area where the tone vibrates. Some are felt more in the chest, others in the mouth, the throat, and the highest notes feel more "heady." Awareness, *not* a conscious physical adjustment, allows the singer to recognize these subtle changes. Again, we turn to the ear for this recognition.

The old singers were divided on whether there were two or three

Every voice is in a sense the result of development, and this is particularly so in my own case. The marble that comes from the quarries of Carrara in Italy may be very beautiful and white and flawless, but it does not shape itself into a work of art without the hand, the heart, and the intellect of the sculptor.

Enrico Caruso – from *The Art of Singing*, by S. Fucito and B.J. Beyer

registers. The consensus now is that there are only two for basses and baritones, and three for the others (refer to the Vocalise section). Each register (or vibrating level) has a different quality of sound; and each register enhances the color of the voice in a different way.

The areas between the low, medium, and high registers are called in Italian, *passaggi*. The terms "register" and "*passaggio*" are both controversial in that all charts vary as to how many there are, where they are, how extended they are, and what to do about them. If you listen, your ear will guide you. You will feel the minute changes throughout the scale. Each voice varies as to where they occur. *But*, if you put your trust only in charts and measurements, you will get what you ask for: mathematical measurements. You will become a mathematician and not a singer!

It will help if you understand that the different registers of the voice are merely modifications in the qualities of tone, or, put another way, in the tone's vibrating level. These modifications come about naturally if there is no conscious interference to the adjustments. Physiologically, they represent different adjustments of the vocal chords or ligaments, and different positions of the larynx.

We will first look at negotiating the passaggi; then we will address how to apply this in order to blend the registers.

Negotiating the Passaggi

A perfectly sung chromatic scale is the true test of the singer's correct "tuning." Observance of half-step intervals is particularly important in the areas of the *passaggio*. Always think the pitch you are singing, not what follows. This is the key to singing "in tune."

The smooth negotiation of the *passaggi* depends on two things:

1)   the singer's ear, and

2)   keen awareness of the intonation on half-steps.

As the ear is refined to recognize these variations in the tone, the whole body will be used as a resonator and the singer will be able to master the use of color.

Returning to the concept of breathing, any undue tension in this act will prevent the voice from seeking its natural vibrating levels.

Also, the tendency to "stretch" or enlarge the distance between one pitch and another is an error. For example, if wrongly conceived, the interval of a third can seem too large.

The negotiation of the *passaggi* depends on acute attention to each pitch. The blending, as you call it, takes place as each adjustment is made. I believe in a "tempered scale."

The smooth negotiation of the *passaggi*, using the ear, and being keenly aware of the intonation on half-steps, also influences the singer's freedom and facility in arriving at the high or the lowest notes.

To smoothly proceed from the low to the medium and then to the high notes in the scale, we also use vowels and timbre. But it is the ear that must be trained to differentiate the components of the sound. The ear is to the singer what the eye is to the painter.

> *You should anticipate delight in hearing your own voice.*
> Clara Doria – from *Your Voice and You*

In the Vocalise section you will find an ideal study for negotiating the passaggi. These are slow, chromatic sequences of no more than five notes in the areas that are identified as passaggi. Allow the throat to adjust as the exercise is done. Attempting to "open the throat," "make space," or lift the soft palate consciously will defeat the purpose of the exercise.

Ascending to High Notes, and Descending

Looking at the high register, note an important principle: The higher the note, the thinner the cords become as they vibrate more rapidly. Any attempt to maintain the same feeling of a more open throat and the width felt in the lower notes will *prevent* the natural action required for the higher pitches.

In other words, for higher notes, the image is that of a more slender sound. Above all there must be no widening of the mouth to accommodate the higher pitches. The "inner smile" spoken of by the Italians is felt *behind* the nose and in the place where the nostrils seem to be open.

If the voice has a muffled sound without much resonance, it helps to intone a sentence or two in a high, childlike voice. I call it the "Snow White, 'Someday My Prince Will Come'" voice! This activates energy and uses the front edges of the cords. It eliminates thickness and gives energy and brightness to the sound.

In ascending scales or intervals the pitch-sound should be visualized with the highest pitch in mind. This does not mean abandoning the calm, contained breath. If left alone, the larynx is higher on low notes and descends for high notes. It is still an *infinitesimal* amount of movement. The advice to keep the larynx low at all times creates havoc with natural sound!

The fear of high notes can be conquered by feeling as if the lower note is the higher pitch and the higher pitch is the lower. The hand can be of help for this image:

Place your hand above your head on the initiation of the lower note, and bring it down as you ascend to the higher pitch. This makes for a smooth ascent and the extremities seem much closer to each other. Do not be tempted to sing every higher note louder, especially if the word is an article. Observe the shape of the whole phrase and the accent of the language within it.

There is a myth I need to dispel: that greater expulsion of breath gives power to high notes. Actually, just the opposite is true! *Less* breath gives higher intensity. This must be coupled with slender, "non-spacing" in the throat. Always think of a high note as slender and as using only a small bit of cord. Initiate the sound with a minimum amount of breath and sing *piano*. Then, quickly increase its volume.

Related to this is another myth I need to dispel: that "to the ear of the singer, the voice should feel the same size all the way up and down the scale." This is wrong! Any attempt to make the voice sound and feel the same size on high notes will cause a spreading of the sound! The correct solution in approaching the higher register is to allow the sensation that the voice is becoming smaller, more slender, and with rounded vowels. The reduction in the length of the vocal cords can then take place naturally. This ensures an easy ascent to the higher voice.

As you descend from higher notes, always think upward and feel as if there is a circular ascending movement above the notes. The main point is to be with each note as you sing it and be careful not to abandon the note when you are in a descending passage. The following diagram illustrates this:

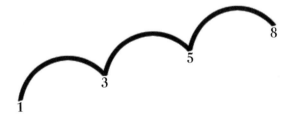

Blending the Registers

The secret to blending the registers is the use of vowel modification. Each vowel has its own characteristics, which vary in color depending on

Shoot for the Moon. Even if you miss it, you will land among the stars.

Les Brown

where it is sung in the scale. However, the basic quality of the voice remains consistent. All five vowels, <u>ah</u>, <u>eh</u>, <u>ee</u>, <u>oh</u>, and <u>oo</u>, should sound equally resonant when sung on any pitch. This requires an adjustment in the phonation. This is addressed in detail in the next chapter, Vowels and Timbre. Examples are also given in charts in the Vocalise section, as well as in the demonstration DVD and CD.

For the purpose of this discussion, we can say that the voice must be "fined-tuned" like any instrument. The ear is the guide. The perceptions become more refined as the singer observes closely the movement from one pitch to another.

One of the most important principles in singing is balance, be it breath versus tone or balance in the body. Rigidity in any form is the enemy of resonance!

Listen for what you sense is your ideal note or pleasing quality. *See* your voice as possessing that quality throughout its entire range.

In conclusion, understand that the changes in pitch, correctly produced, do not result in an obvious change in different parts of the voice. The demands of the music, text, and emotion govern the action of the vocal mechanism, aided by certain vowel modifications, in the highest and lowest parts of the range. It is often said that "you must sing as you speak." I take this to mean the natural spontaneity with which we speak without the necessity of "placing," "directing," or "manipulating" the throat to produce sound. The ideal result is a voice at the service of *musical expression*!

Vowels and Timbre

Conceiving of Vowels and Tone as One Sound

Music is a language all its own, and singing is the "speaking" of it. We could also say that tone is reflected speech. Considering singing this way, it should come as no surprise that the vowel and the tone should be conceived as *one sound*. They are not two different processes.

However, we are taught to strive for perfect diction and the tendency is to consciously form the vowels in the mouth. This causes the tongue to be the activator and does not allow the impulse of sound to start at the glottis, or vocal valve. And if a clear ideal of the vowel and pitch are not united as one, as mentally conceived, there is no clear initiation of the sound. Presetting the tongue and the jaw before singing allows the tongue to control the breath, and the sound is unnatural; it is *tongue* and not *tone*!

Tuned by the ear, each vowel has its own characteristics and may vary in color depending on where it is in the scale (a high, medium, or low note). Nevertheless, the basic quality of the voice remains consistent. The ideal sound is one in which there is a similarity in all the vowels as produced. They seem close to each other and there is no obvious distance between an open and a closed sound. For example, i and eh are bright, ah is more neutral,

The ideal of an artist is to be recognized for the timbre of his voice.

Trans. A. Bach – from
Il Bel Canto,
by Vittorio Ricci

and <u>o</u> and <u>oo</u> are dark. The progression from <u>i</u> to <u>oo</u> should have a similar quality.

The five vowels, <u>ah</u>, <u>eh</u>, <u>ee</u>, <u>oh</u>, and <u>oo</u>, should sound *equally resonant* when sung on any pitch. This requires an adjustment in the *phonation*. Let's look at several examples:

- *On the <u>oo</u> in "boon," the larynx is a bit lower than on the <u>oh</u> in "go."*
- *On an <u>aa</u> like the word "bath," we sense the sound more in the throat.*
- *On <u>eh</u> as in the word "say," the feeling is higher and there is a sense of more narrowness in the throat.*
- *The <u>ee</u> as in "deep" seems to leave little space in the throat. It feels more closed.*

Mental Vowel Shaping

The shape of the vowel is directly responsible for the vibration and beauty of the sound. To attempt to adjust the sound through diction alone is to do the impossible, given the different pitches required in vocal music requiring a long vocal range. I stress that vowel modification is vowel *shaping*, that is, a rounding of the vowel. It must be done *mentally*—never physically—because it is sure to be overdone in some way. No one can determine this through conscious physical adjustments in the process.

This brings to mind a myth I need to dispel—that "good pronunciation is dependent on knowing where the tongue should be on each vowel setting." This is wrong. It is impossible to sing naturally while controlling the muscles in order to enunciate clearly. This practice directs the mind away from the *real* work…HEARING. How, then, is the sound effected? By mentally and automatically seeking the slenderest adjustment in the rounding of the vowel: as the pitch rises, the ear causes the pharyngeal cavity and larynx to adjust perfectly to the pitch.

In contrast, if the vowel is unmodified, as in everyday speech, the pitch, as it rises to the high range, will not allow the cords to undergo the thinning process and tighter occlusion necessary for high notes. It will not allow the cords maximum closure.

The lips can also be an impediment to mental vowel shaping. Any tension or protrusion of the lips on higher pitches causes distortion and woofiness, or hollow tones. The ear informs the mind of what you desire (from sense memory), and the mind carries out the demand, translating it into tone, IF you do not manipulate the lips (or the diaphragm, tongue, jaw, etc.).

Think UPRIGHT or "SU" in Italian when you begin to sing…no matter what vowel you are pronouncing. This prevents the "control" of the lips in forming the vowel.

A danger signal for the singer is when "how does it feel?" becomes primary and physical manipulations and adjustments "take over," forgetting that the ear—not physical demands—is the true gauge for the sound.

The lips must not protrude too much in order to avoid a sound that is too dark (cupo)…neither should the lips be held tightly against the teeth.
Delle Sedie – *Vocal Art*

Vowel shaping in relation to pitch is the golden key to technique.
Herbert Caesari – *The Alchemy of Voice*

Vowel Modification

In order to acquire evenness in the movement from one vowel to another, the singer must understand that vowel modification is *indispensable* to the production of beautiful sound. The modification varies with each vowel, and since each voice is unique in itself, it is the ear of the singer that must be the final judge of the degree of modification of each vowel. This may seem very difficult to comprehend when it is first introduced to the singer, but several simple experiments are worth a thousand words:

Try singing the vowel ee, as in "deep," throughout your range. Note that it is easy to sing in the middle section of the voice, but on lower tones, it must be thought to approach ih, as in "dip." On the lowest notes of the voice (the so-called chest register) the ee is modified further to approach the German word "grüss" umlaut sound. This modification allows the tone to be consistent in its color and beauty and gives the voice timbre (color) as well as a smooth sound.

Now try singing the vowel oo, as in "stoop," throughout your range. Again, this vowel sound is favorable to the middle voice, but on ascending the scale it becomes oo, as in "foot."

We ordinarily speak in a much more limited range than when we sing, and consequently, we are unaware of changes. But try singing a B flat (or another very high note in your range) on a pure ee vowel. This is sure to cause strain and stridency in the sound!

A ventriloquist is able to make the vowels distinguishable without opening the mouth widely. The singer who is having difficulty pronouncing words on higher pitches would do well to first whisper them and then breathe and sing. This will reduce the temptation to rise off the sound column itself in an attempt to "place the voice" for the high note.

Become aware of the subtle changes in the vowels in all ranges of your voice. You will become aware of their "place" without *placing* them. Technique will ultimately become involuntary and this will give wings to your creativity. For all notes, it is sometimes helpful to *think* a silent H before introducing the tone.

Another important principle is to open the mouth in a consistent manner for all vowels. If instead the singer adjusts the opening to narrow for ee, to very small and round for oh, and to long and wide for ah, he or she will surely allow the tongue to control, and not the impetus from the glottal valve.

> *I often suggest that the singer place a finger on his chin. No, this is not to push down or hold down the jaw; it is merely to become aware that the ee, eh, ah, oh, and oo can be intoned with the same aperture of the mouth. Any inordinate changes in the opening of the jaw indicate to me that the singer is unable to refine the sounds into a consistent quality. It will be observed that when the finger is lightly placed there, it discourages unnatural "mouthing" of the tone and the diaphragm will be activated in the correct manner of supporting the sound.*

This should convince you that the vowels are formed primarily in the throat. The Italians say, *cantare nel ghorgo*. The variations in the shape of the mouth which accompany production are secondary. The more sounds are consciously "mouthed" in an attempt to project the voice, the more they are deprived of the natural color and timbre of the voice. Again, the result is *tongue* and not *tone*. Each vowel must be mentally conceived as incorporated in the pitch itself.

Timbre, Phonation, and Harmonics

A singer's sound is determined mainly by the type of voice—soprano, mezzo soprano, contralto, tenor, baritone, and bass. But the *timbre*, or color, of the voice is dependent on the characteristics of the sound in *phonation*, or the manner in which the tone and pitch are united.

Sounds can be described by many adjectives. Below are some of those frequently used by Italians to describe voices:

Suoni luminosi	luminous sounds
Tenebrosi	dark, without light
Duri	hard
Morbidi	soft
Pastosi	soft, fluid (like pasta)
Aspri	bitter, penetrating
Vellutati	velvety
Mordenti	biting

Now a word about the harmonics of a sound—the *armonici*. Every sound is composed of a fundamental and the harmonics surrounding it. The harmonics are the overtones that result when the fundamental sound is clearly produced. The success of the singer depends on his keen awareness that the true tuning of the voice depends on the clear concept of the pitch and vowel as one, without attempting to adjust the throat for volume.

A thick loud sound without the center, as it were—the fine adjustment mentioned above—does not carry, and is mainly heard by the singer and not the audience. Often the smaller voice has much more vocal presence and carrying power by virtue of its slender sound. When I speak of a slender sound, I mean one in which the vocal cords close naturally without attempting to make the sound broader or more dense in color than is genuine to the particular voice. Trying to "open the throat," "make space" in the throat, and consciously manipulating the soft palate destroys the fundamental sound and, hence, the harmonics or overtones are diminished.

Vowel Scale versus Vocal Scale

There is a seeming conflict between the vowel scale and the musical scale. If the music calls for you to sing a high note on <u>oo</u>, how do you proceed? If the <u>oo</u> is maintained in its purest spoken form, the natural resonation cannot occur.

The knowledge of the vowel modification, if *mentally conceived*, makes the involuntary adjustment for ideal resonation. This is also true of <u>ee</u> when sung on low pitches. See the graph of Doria in the Vocalise section. Conceive the pitch and vowel as one musical sound, single and indivisible!

Vowels *can* be formed in the mouth and *only there* can they be shaped voluntarily and directly. But the result will be that the vowels, while they may be understood, will lack the substance and real quality that can only be obtained when activated at the base of the throat. Whispering the vowels gives the feeling as to where this occurs. *You cannot intentionally shape vowels when you whisper*!

The space above the larynx is an adjustable resonator. It varies as the space is activated by the pitch of the primary tone initiated at the glottis (valve). Deaf mutes are taught to speak knowing the exact positions of speech as controlled in the mouth. The sounds they make are proof that the true beauty of the voice does not originate there.

Here is a test to prove the above:

> *Open your mouth easily (moderately open) and place your finger on your chin.* Do not *push down or put pressure on the chin in any way. Next, whisper* <u>ah</u>, <u>eh</u>, <u>ee</u>, <u>oh</u>, <u>oo</u>. *Now sing these same vowels on a medium pitch. Notice how little the face changes. No pouting of the lips on* <u>oo</u> *...only a gentle rounding of the mouth.*

As I keep repeating, this is the secret of beautiful sound. The pitch and the vowel are one sound, single and undivided.

As we are talking about the shaping of the mouth, I should point out that the consensus of all the great maestri of the past is that the opening of the mouth is a very important factor in achieving beautiful sounds. However, widening the mouth produces white sounds. The ideal opening is *vertical*.

Consonants and Articulation

The art of articulation is separate and distinct from vocalizing. Why? Because all consonants are formed in the mouth, and all vocal sounds proceed or should proceed from the throat. The consonant is a momentary closure or obstruction to the vocal sound. They are two separate acts. The consonant is a door, if you will. It shuts off the breath and opens to allow the voice to come through. The retaining of breath is a *mental act*—it is taken in stillness and remains stationary until either the consonant is pronounced or the vowel is initiated at the glottis…by imagining the pitch and vowel as *one*.

As noted earlier, any tension in the lips, especially in the upper lip, produces stiffness in the sound. The production of consonants using the lips must be done with lightning swiftness and not forceful expulsion of air.

There are three types of consonants:

1. Percussive: P, T, K, and Ch

   These are merely positions of the tongue and lips that close and open. *Example: whisper lightly the vowels after concentrating on the percussive as present only in the mouth* (pip, tent, tut, kick, cork, church).

2. Sonants: B, D, G, V, J, Z, Zh, Th (as in "thy"), and R

   These are murmurs heard only when pronounced in

Now, a singer can never allow the facial expression to alter the position of the jaw or mouth. Facial expression for the singer must concern itself chiefly with the eyes and forehead…too wide a smile often accompanies what is called 'the white voice.' This is a voice production where a head resonance alone is employed, without sufficient appoggio or enough of the mouth to give the tone a vital quality.

Luisa Tetrazzini – from *The Art of Singing*, by S. Fucito and B.J. Beyer

conjunction with the vowel (bub, babe, did, dude, gig,

gag, vive, verve, judge, ziz, there, with, rare).

3. Whispered: F, S, Th (as in "thin"), Sh, Wh, and H

These are heard independently from the voice (fife,

sea, sheet, hush, think, faith, which, whoo, hall).

The idea is to not permit the thought of the tonal pitch to take place before preceding consonants. I think it is helpful to say that the consonants must be whispered on the bar line or musical rest preceding the sound to be vocalized.

See the graph of consonant division from Doria in the Vocalise section. It will be helpful to think of the consonants above the mentally shaped vowels. The consonant is separate and must be precise. The consonant must also be a mental demand. On low pitches this sensation can be felt; on high pitches, it is felt hardly at all. There is more compression on the lips when followed by low notes, particularly with consonants such as B, P, and M.

The essence of the artist is that he should be articulate.

A. C. Swinburne

Remember to use only the air in the mouth for consonants. The higher you sing, the less you will feel the sensation of the consonant.

I often say to my singers, your high notes will never feel broad, velvety, or as full as you might wish to have them. If they do, only you hear them and they are probably throaty. If you are in doubt, listen to yourself on a tape. Sometimes singers will say their high notes sound white and reedy, without beauty. They are then amazed at the resonant sound they hear on tape. Why? It is because the chords are allowed to vibrate as a result of the clear intention for the desired pitch without being overblown with air pressure or the mistaken idea of making space in the throat, which gives a false impression of the sound produced.

Consonants with Vowels

The articulation of the consonant must be complete before voicing the vowel, bearing in mind that the consonant is articulated in the mouth and the vowel in the glottis.

Clara Doria – *English Diction in Song and Speech*

This section would be incomplete without an overall statement about the place of consonants in conjunction with vowels. Clear articulation of consonants is dependent on the understanding that it is only the breath in the mouth, not any from the lungs, that gives clarity to diction.

It may seem difficult to imagine, but all consonants occurring at the beginning or middle of a word cause an interruption of the flow of breath from the lungs. When mastered, there is no obvious break in the flow of sound.

> *Vowels are initiated in the larynx. Consonants remain the "whispered" reflection in the mouth. Any attempt to produce vowels consciously in the mouth cuts off the flow of air through the cords. The result is tongue pressure, not the free-flowing bel canto sound.*

There is a myth I need to dispel: that "the consonant and the vowel are initiated in the same action or place." The result makes it seem so, but in reality, the consonant should be felt and take place as if on top of the vowel. The mere whispering of the consonant and then immediately singing the vowel will illustrate this.

Legato

The Italian word *legare* means to "tie together." The all important style of *legato* is a principle that is associated with bel canto—the smooth flow from one note to another without interruptions. If you hum on a low pitch, the sensation of continuity is what is felt in *legato* singing. It is a feeling of droning. The overtone from one note to another makes a circle over to the next sound.

It is very difficult to put into words the explanation of *legato*. It is better demonstrated on the recordings. However, the feeling of slow motion aids in understanding and acquiring a true *legato*. The breath should not be affected by variations in pitch. It is steady and constant. The ability to move easily from one *tone* to another is dependent on the smooth transitions from one *pitch* to another. The effect of *legato* singing depends on the singer's ability to sustain one note until the next is sung.

An essential principle is the holding of the notes and the binding of them one to another. Who does not have this skill does not sing.

Trans. Lamperti – from *Il Bel Canto*, by Vittorio Ricci

 The practice of legato *should be initiated with a few notes sung slowly. The smoothest liberation of the sound should be felt as a sustained hum. Whether the music calls for slow or quick movement,* arpeggios, *or a trill in florid music, the effect is the same as a long sustained note.*

A simple exercise I have recently found helpful is one from a book by Jean-Pierre Blivet, the teacher of Natalie Dessay, a marvelous French soprano. In it he says, "One must recognize the value of *not* working on single vowels...The "or" stimulates the area of the pharynx, the "oh" allows the pharynx to remain normal, without pushing it down, and the "oui" brings out the "sharpness," meaning the "sheen.""* Here is the exercise:

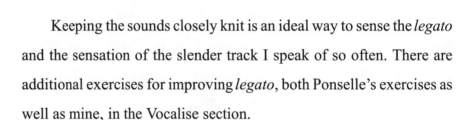

Sing five tones descending on the vowels OR-OH-OUI, that is, "or-oh" and the French "oui."

Keeping the sounds closely knit is an ideal way to sense the *legato* and the sensation of the slender track I speak of so often. There are additional exercises for improving *legato*, both Ponselle's exercises as well as mine, in the Vocalise section.

Portamento

The art of *portamento* is another description used by the masters. It means, literally, "carrying" the sound, or carrying one tone over to another. It is, in fact, the procession from one note to another with an almost imperceptible move through each intermediate pitch.

There are several examples in the Vocalise section. See the exercise on octave down "padre" and the opening phrase of "Mi Chiamano Mimì." These must be executed without driving for a big crescendo.

Within each sound there is an almost imperceptible change in the volume. It is this fluidity that gives the voice a true *legato*. A teacher of mine from La Scala used to compare the movement from one note to

Volume is ONE...only the intensity changes. Dynamically a piano and a forte...are produced with equal support. The forte does not mean to open the throat and the piano doesn't require lessening the space in the throat.

Dick Marzollo (Master coach of Cesare Siepi)

* Jean-Pierre Blivet, *La Voie du Chant* (Paris: Librarie Arthème Fayard, 1999).

another to a strand of pearls. Each sound is completed before going on to the next. In the case of a *portamento*, the tone should be diminished before the upward or downward glide. Otherwise, it becomes a "moanamento" rather than a true *portamento*. The tone should always be considered a part of the phrase meant to convey a certain emphasis on the text.

Another important aid to maintaining a good *legato* is to mentally accent tied notes. This preserves the rhythmic sense of the music and ensures that the sound continues through the tie. The idea of "bowing" a *legato* phrase has an immediate effect. I encourage singers to think of themselves as violinists who produce continuity of sound through the bow on their strings.

Sustained and Repeated Notes

Without body of tone even the finest pianissimo has no significance.
Lilli Lehmann – *How to Sing*

To maintain the flow of a sustained note, the thought should reinforce the pitch through *mental* repetition, and if the thought of a silent "N" is added to the last word in a long phrase ending on "ah," thus becoming "annnn" in thought ONLY, it will ensure a clarity and a smooth ending to the sound.

Repeating notes on one pitch in a syncopated tempo gives a feeling of flow and implements the freedom in *legato* singing. However, repeated notes also can be a hindrance to the phrase. It is helpful to conceive of repeated notes as being successively a bit higher. This avoids vocal fatigue, and it also keeps the tone from spreading and becoming heavy. Attention to the important accent of the word or words in each is also a more relaxed way of singing through them.

Messa di Voce

Messa di voce is the technique of increasing the volume in a note and then decreasing it. As in all aspects of bel canto, every principle is involved. The *appoggio*, or the initiation of the sound, is the means for developing the *messa di voce*. This is not to forsake the sense of the "hum" or "drone" in the sound. Setting the throat in anticipation of the sound causes the sound to be thick and unwieldy. I cannot stress too often the idea of a clear intention of the pitch and vowel united as one thought. (See Delle Sedie, Vocalise section.)

The true study of *messa di voce* depends on the keen visualization of the tone's initiation, expansion, and the gradual diminishing of it. Here are several aids to developing *messa di voce*:

- First, it helps to think of the tone in beats 1...2...3...4... etc.

- Secondly, an aid to diminishing the sound is to perceive of it as if it is rising to a higher and then a higher octave.

- When singing a phrase that begins with a consonant, you must be aware that the consonant is a separate act and precedes the initiation of the sound.

- The mark of *forte* in a score does not mean a vocal explosion of force. The true idea of bel canto is a rapier-like initiation of the sound, and immediately after, a reinforcement of the sound, or a diminishment, as the phrase indicates.

Rosa Ponselle is a shining example of the use of *legato* and the *messa di voce*. Her voice had the haunting color of *chiaro-scuro*. Ponselle's recently released recordings made late in life at her home in Stevenson, Maryland, ("Villa Pace") are made at close range and are just as I remember hearing her when I was fortunate to study with her there. In a room her voice seemed very slender in its approach to sound—not noisy in volume, but with a pure beauty of tone without weightiness. Ponselle's voice was like a slender thread being drawn through a needle—always pliable, and it was possible to "feel" the hum or drone I have spoken about.

A crescendo in a phrase must be linked to emotion. The energy comes about as a result of the meaning of the text. The sound must always be initiated with the greatest precision...lightly and *not* by degrees. Diminishing the size of the sound is the *willed* desire to decrease the breath pressure until the singer chooses to end the sound.

Imagery plays a big part in this skill. In fact, the singer is called to develop his sense of beauty in the sound through the conscious use of the poetic, the imagination, and the artistic intuition that are as important to exercise as the vocal exercises themselves.

In diminishing a tone, the throat remains the same. Only the quantity of breath given forth is diminished.

Luisa Tetrazzini – from *The Art of Singing*, by S. Fucito and B. J. Beyer

Agility

True bel canto grew out of the style of florid singing developed in the seventeenth and eighteenth centuries. Clarity of execution in this style is often confused with the deliberate separation of every note, with the result sounding like HA-HA-HA. But it is actually *smoothness* that is the true key to agility, and the ability to clearly execute phrases.

Agility can only be mastered *after* the singer has acquired the co-ordination of the breath with the sound itself. I have included some exercises in the Vocalise section. When beginning to study agility, small groups of notes are sung, *not* inordinately long passages.

Rubini and Lablache were the famous tenor and bass who sang the first performances of Bellini's operas. I found their exercise books on singing when I lived in Paris. You will find some of these exercises in the Vocalise section, as well as a few exercises on *legato* and *cadenzas* by Marietta Brambilla, a famous contralto of that time. I have included dates and information about them.

To attempt to sing florid passages in a fast tempo before the notes are learned can only lead to control by manipulating the throat, the

Agility is essential for the artistic singer from the point of view of elasticity and softness (pliability) as well as the style of bravura (brilliant singing).
Delle Sedie –
Vocal Art

lips, and the tongue. The passages you are singing must be learned slowly and rhythmically at first. Observe the patterns, where the vowels and the words fit, as well as the proper accents.

By repeating the notes first mentally, then slowly singing them, the ear seizes the pattern and, like a computer, logs it in. Only then should you increase the passage to the correct tempo.

To sing with agility the singer should emit just a small amount of air, with the mouth opened only partly. The final sensation while singing florid music is akin to a smooth glide, supported by a constant hum. Finally, pitch changes are controlled by the ear calling forth the breath, *not* by neck control and tongue.

Staccato

The study of staccato is very important to the acquisition of true agility. I have included several exercises in my own vocalises. The support feels minimal; in fact, the less air used the better. The sensation is gentle, well supported (lightly), and notice that as one sound is completed, a suction causes the breath to be available instantaneously.

A magnificent example of staccato singing can be heard in Callas' recording of the "Shadow Song" from DINORAH. She is able to repeat patterns both in full voice and, immediately following, in *piano*, which has the effect of an echo.

In the exercises and explanations in the Vocalise section by another great vocal master, Delle Sedie, it is apparent that many vocal effects are achieved by imagery related to sound. Delle Sedie has a whole book of exercises on vocal timbres relating to emotions. He uses poetry to develop the singer's ability to generate real emotion in the sound of the voice.

When one wishes to sing agility or pianissimo, it is necessary to emit the smallest amount of air (un filo di voce). The mouth is semi-opened. Passing from pianissimo to mezzo-forte you need only to augment the amount of air without changing anything in the throat.

Trans. M. Garcia – from *Il Bel Canto*, by Vittorio Ricci

Agility must be studied slowly.

Lamperti – *The Art of Singing*

Phrasing

Every phrase must be a new beginning. Each has a definite shape. It can be visualized. Its color is determined by the word, the tempo, and the dynamic accents it requires. With this conception, there is never a standard, repeated, predictable performance by the singer.

It is helpful to determine a "median" note in a phrase. It should be like the center from which you move up and down the scale. It can be likened to a "see-saw." The board moves up and down from a center point. This center "median" is constant and balances the voice in color and texture as it moves up and down the scale.

Manuel Garcia noted that agility ascending is more difficult than in descending. "The voice, in ascending, slows down the sound, and on the contrary, it moves fast in descending. These two defects can be corrected by giving equal force to all the notes, which will then be perfectly distinct and *legato*."*

> *If a phrase or tone is difficult, try dancing while mentally hearing the music. It will release undue tension and bring greater ease to the sounds. Your ear is to you like the eye of the painter, but you have to sharpen your ear with concentrated purpose. The ideal is to achieve the maximum result with the minimum of effort.*

The courage to take a different look at tone and phrase—the whole, whether through movement, dialogue, or reflection—is the requirement for growth. I have witnessed great strides in true communicativeness in singers, who, at the beginning of their studies were seemingly

* Vittorio Ricci, *Il Bel Canto* (Milan: Hoepli, 1923)

limited both vocally and musically. This took place through their decision to risk the unknown—the new note in their range and the new concept of the pursuit of the challenge.

Let the Maestro know that it is better to have a pupil sing in a moderate tempo than to sing fast passages in which he has not time to organize himself. This leads to mediocrity, and through the negligence of the Maestro, the pupil will get worse.

Trans. Tosi – from
Il Bel Canto, by
Vittorio Ricci

Recitatives and Cadenzas

Recitatives

The word *recitative* literally means "recited." The charm and the appeal of the many sung recitatives in the bel canto repertoire particularly depend on the natural accents of the words—much like the dialogue of an actor. Though divided into bars with the notes interspersed with rests, the recitative must sound as free as if spoken. All good Italian composers fit the accents of the language into the composition of their recitatives. Recitatives are important for setting the scenes, through comedy or dramatic accents, for the concerted music that follows.

Too often singers will neglect the recitative, resulting in a decline in the quality of the script. For example, some singers pace recitatives so quickly that they make no sense. Others leave out all natural accents of the language and the recitatives become "sing-songy" and boring.

From a rare book named *Il Bel Canto*, by Vittorio Ricci, a study of bel canto with quotations from all the great maestri of the seventeenth and eighteenth centuries, I quote a few of the defects of many singers when singing recitatives, as described by P. F. Tosi,* one of the most

A singer possessing a beautiful voice, but without intelligence, will always be inferior to one with a mediocre voice and high intelligence.

Trans. Panofka – from *L'Arte del Canto*

---

* Tosi's book, *Observations on a Florid Song*, was originally published in Italian in 1743. It was translated and published in London by Wm. Reeves Bookseller, Ltd. in 1926.

famous teachers of singing. They are amusing and certainly call out the most common defects that are heard even today!

Free translation: "There are those who sing the recitatives as if in church...there are those who bark, who seem to sing in secret or confusion...those who accent the last syllable or leave it off...some who devour them...others don't pronounce or express anything...they laugh, cry, screech and often sing flat...the worst part is that they do not feel the need to correct these errors."

I advocate speaking the text of the recitative without singing it, at first. This is the means to awareness of the accent of the language. It is helpful to listen to Shakespeare. His brilliant use of words is a challenge to the actor. It is no less important for the singer to put meaning and color into the recitatives.

Cadenzas

Cadenzas are the musical enhancements to arias. Their color and meaning must grow out of the text of the aria. They must have a musical shape even if they seem to be mere vocal flights. If the *cadenzas* display only technical ability without any emotional relationship to the music and plot, they become meaningless, shallow displays designed to draw applause only for their brilliant execution.

I studied with a marvelous coach from La Scala who had been the maestro backstage in charge of all music sung offstage and entrances and exits of singers at La Scala during all the triumphs of Callas. He opened my eyes to the *andamento*—the tempo and movement necessary to give the *cadenza* a strong statement. It is a matter of dynamics and shaping of the phrasing to maximize the beauty of the whole.

Through flexibility and morbidezza (lightness, softness) the serious singer will acquire the necessary inflections to show sentiment, to paint the situations with logic and truth and to give the phrases appropriate color which it is meant to express.

Delle Sedie – *Vocal Art*

I suggest you listen to how Callas shapes a *cadenza*. A good example is at the end of the first part of the aria "Al Dolce Guidami" in ANNA BOLENA. Another wonderful *cadenza* is sung by Ileana Cotrubas at the end of the aria "Comme Autre Fois" in Bizet's LES PECHEURS DE PERLES. Of course, it is easy to find many such examples in the early recordings of Domingo, Bergonzi, or Von Stade, as well as in the recordings of Pavarotti, the baritone Bryn Terfel, and Freni.

There are exercises in the Vocalise section for practicing *cadenzas*.

Part 2

Voice Freedom

A rare book of collected comments by all the most
esteemed teachers of bel canto.

Discovering Your Voice

Discovering your voice is perhaps the most significant part of being a singer. Your voice is your creation—the sound and accompanying message you want to project. This message is the way to communicate the music to your audience with your voice, your imagery, your emotions. You discover your voice by learning to listen to your own voice, by listening to other singers, and by *freeing yourself to become* the type of singer you want to be and to embrace the role you want to sing.

In order to hear your voice you need feedback, and you need role models—in other words, you need to know *where you are now*, so that you can understand what you need to do to be *where you want to be*. Recall what Rossini said was the requirement for an ideal singer, mentioned in the Introduction: "A naturally beautiful voice, even throughout its range, careful training that encouraged effortless delivery of highly florid music, and a mastery of style *that could only be assimilated from listening to the best Italian exponents.*" (Emphasis added.)

In Part 4, I list many of the best role models to listen to. But first you need to learn that most essential vocal technique: how to train your voice with the ear.

First of all, singing must be natural. Any forcing, any effort that involves the least strain on the vocal apparatus (whether it be an effort for range, for power, for endurance, for anything at all) is sure to have an unwholesome effect.

Ebe Stignani -
Etude Magazine
interview

Training Your Voice with the Ear

The results singers can expect are only as good as their conceptions of what is a beautiful sound. The ear of the teacher is of great importance in helping the student find gratifying and consistent sounds. Some of these qualities are clarity, luminosity, radiance, musicality, and communication.

The teacher points out the direction to the student by indicating to him his best sounds. For example, to correct a wiry tremulous tone, the teacher might offer the image of a more rounded "closed" tone. A too breathy tone is corrected by mentally demanding that singing be done with a minimal amount of air to produce the sound.

I found that all my teachers in Italy were able either to illustrate what they considered my best tones or to suggest listening to great singers in the theaters or through recordings. Above all, the Italian maestri stress that all sounds should seem to emanate from one place… not the feeling of height or reaching for high notes or for low notes as well. This is achieved through the study of vowel modification, which is also a "mental imaging."

The Italian maestro also relies on his ear in teaching. While studying in Paris, I worked with Maria Castellazzi-Bovy, an Italian soprano who had sung for years at La Scala. In Milan, one of my favorite coaches was the conductor Alfredo Strano, who was a pupil of Ciléa in composition. The approach of both Castellazzi-Bovy and Strano was to make me aware of my best, most simple, natural sounds and to attempt to produce them evenly throughout the voice.

The term *morbidezza* was constantly used. It means softness and warmth, as opposed to "driven" sounds. *Chiaro-scuro* is the term used to imply that the voice must have both light and dark tints to be a perfect sound. Mere technique was never the scope of the singer. It was the

I should say that the Italian vocal teacher teaches first of all, with his ears. He listens with the greatest possible intensity to every shade of tone-color until his ideal tone reveals itself. Possibly the worst kind of a vocal teacher is the one who has some set plan or device or theory which must be followed "willy-nilly" in order that the teacher's theories may be vindicated. With such a teacher no voice is safe.

Pasquale Amato – *Great Singers on the Art of Singing*, by J.F. Cooke

communication of beauty through feelings, emotions, and the urgency to express the composer's music.

You must become the master of your own voice ultimately, but you will need two other ears that you trust. The teacher's ear is the first requisite for helping the singer. Your voice must be a reflection of you, *not your teacher*. Become keenly aware of the counsel you receive, then strain it through the ear and not the eye.

I am convinced that the singer who is truly committed to his creative growth will find vocal and artistic solutions for himself. The guidelines of the teacher are just that; they are guidelines and not boundaries.

Listening to Other Singers

Many teachers of singing and singers are not advocates of listening to other performers because of the temptation to imitate. My feelings about this are different since my first teacher told me to listen to several singers who could form my taste in sound and style. These were Caruso, Tito Schipa, and Rosa Ponselle. I firmly believe that my sense of sound and style have always been influenced by hearing recordings of live singers in concert or opera.

The teaching I received in Italy and France was based on hearing how the teacher approached sound. I had already had this experience with Rosa Ponselle, with whom I had a few lessons, and also in coaching with Lotte Lehmann. Training the ear to follow the vowel progression, as well as the overall concept of style in recording, can be, in my opinion, of great value.

Be sure to include the early recordings when you listen to great singers. One important aspect of the earlier recordings is the participation of conductors who were nearer to the composers of the time. Puccini,

My feeling is that reputation or "method" can sometimes be a doubtful guide. The final test is how good a teacher is for you. If you, your voice, and your singing feel natural, unconstricted, and sort of buoyed up by your teacher's care, the chances are that you have the right one for you (which doesn't at all mean that he is the right teacher for your best friend!) and when you have found such a teacher, stay with him and have confidence in him.

Robert Merrill – Etude Magazine Interview

Mascagni, and Strauss all had these benefits. A prime example of a singer who lived close to the time Bellini composed his operas was Adelina Patti, who was advanced in age in her last recording of "Ah, non credea" from his SONNAMBULA. Lilli Lehmann sang many Wagner roles, and Lotte Lehmann and Maria Jeritza created roles in the operas of Puccini and Strauss.

Listening to early recordings takes a willingness to accept the fact that the recording industry was in its infancy at the time. However, there are producers like Marston who are able to reveal the true sound of the voice through remastering the original disks.

To listen to great conductors of various operas is also very important. In the Italian operatic repertoire there are complete operas conducted by De Sabata, Mugnone, and Toscanini; and later Serafin, Abbado, and Sinopoli. George Prêtre is exemplary in the French repertoire, while Furtwängler, Bruno Walter, Kleiber, and Böhm are important, as was von Karajan.

I sang with De Fabritiis on several occasions in the late 1960s, and although he was never considered in the class of the aforementioned, he recorded many operas with singers in the 1940s and 50s, as well as later.

In the field of song literature (*lieder*) there are many interesting recordings for research. The series called *The Hugo Wolf Society* is very informative and indicative of Wolf's ideas for interpretation. Lotte Lehmann has many interesting recordings of Schubert, Brahms, and Schumann with Bruno Walter at the piano. Other fine singers of songs are Thomas Hampson, Thomas Allen, Anne Sophie von Otter, Monica Groop, and Dawn Upshaw, as well as Bryn Terfel and Thomas Quasthoff. Of course, the singing of Cecilia Bartoli is a very specialized art and her research on early music is notable.

A teacher of singing must be, or must have been, a good singer. It is not enough that he should have mixed with or heard good singers, or have accompanied them either as orchestral conductor or on the pianoforte or other instrument; such experiences may give him an insight into the effects an artiste can produce, but they will afford him none into the means by which these effects are produced.

Sir Charles Santley –
The Art of Singing

I try to hear most of the new singers in person in order to better understand their voices. With all the recording science of today, it is easy to make a lyric tenor sing a repertoire that is too heavy and demanding—a repertoire that would be very damaging in a live theater performance. I feel that both Di Stefano and Carreras made the mistake of singing roles that were not suited to them on recordings, and were fooled into thinking that the dramatic roles suited them. They both paid a high vocal price. Von Karajan was forever enticing singers to sing heavier roles for him!

Applying These Vocal Principles to Popular Music

I primarily use examples from opera throughout this book, because it is the most all-encompassing, dramatic, and challenging vocal music there is. However, as you "discover your voice," you may discover that you want to sing popular music, either all the time or some of the time. This section of the book is addressed to you specifically, to help you apply these principles to the multitudinous forms of popular music, from folk to rock to musical comedy.

First of all, the ideal singer has a healthy vocal instrument. One of my goals is to help the singer achieve vocal longevity.

The main difference between classical singing and popular singing is the use of breath to produce sound. The classical approach relies on the gentle use of the breath to send out the sound, allowing it to be nourished by the resonance chambers, while the so-called "pop" singer relies on the microphone for vocal projection. The pop artist relies on diction and forced dramatic accents, putting direct pressure on the cords as if speaking, without flow of breath to send out the sound.

In the classical style, there are the head and chest resonances. Evenness of sound depends on the use of the breath. Instead, the popular singer

In the very beginning singers must realize that their art is something they must acquire for themselves. The teacher is an aide, an assistant, but the real work of true advancement remains with the pupil. Singing is the most legitimate of arts: no one else can put in a touch with brush or pencil for one; one must face it alone.

Lillian Nordica –
Hints to Singers

People don't go to 'hear' an opera anymore. They go to 'see' an opera. When production is the almighty god, the more opulent and gimmicky it can be, the more it's touted as supreme. It seems as though the stage directors and the designers are the first people signed up anymore, and then as an afterthought, they say, "Oh, yes, now we need singers."

Mirella Freni – Interview, *Opera Monthly*, Dec. 1994

relies on the "so-called" chest quality throughout the entire range, as high as possible in the individual voice. Usually there is a very obvious switch to a headier sound. Those who rely exclusively on what is known as a "belt" sound, such as Mariah Carey and Aretha Franklin, put enormous pressure on their vocal cords. They scream, shriek, and do death defying leaps in pitch. When Whitney Houston was at the beginning of her career the most outstanding quality was her blend, but her voice steadily diminished as a result of her unhealthy vocal choices.

On the other hand, there are many great vocalists who are able to use the chest voice mixed with head resonance even though the chest resonance is dominant. Examples of this type of singer are Barbra Streisand and Linda Eder. The Broadway style is geared toward the "belt," as it is called. The only singer of this type I remember who could be heard without amplification in all parts of the theater was Ethel Merman. I was always in awe of her, but judged from a classical standpoint, it was "vocal death." And then there are the stylists who impress with text, and sing with rasps, twangy and strained vibration, and noise. Janis Joplin may have been a phenomenon to some, but I would hardly remember her voice for its beauty! Britney Spears captivates us with her youth, but I wonder how this style will serve her and others of her generation before nodes and polyps create completely dysfunctional voices.

The country western singers sing better for the most part than the other popular vocalists. They usually are concerned with telling a story and attempt to convey real meaning to the text.

Of course, there are exceptional singers in all styles—for example, the phenomenal, intuitive singing of Ella Fitzgerald. She could sing like an instrument in her "scat" style with unlimited range and spontaneity, and then sing a ballad with great simplicity. Cleo Laine is another singer of this type.

Audra McDonald is another singer who is equally at home in opera and popular music. She has won awards for her performance in Terence McNally's MASTER CLASS about Maria Callas. She performed the very difficult opening aria of Lady Macbeth from Verdi's opera, MACBETH, and has also won awards for her Broadway appearances.

Celine Dion is another performer who is able to sing in a wide range, and her communicative ability allows her to be very effective. She, like many singers, is highly intuitive and I am sure she has come to her technique through experience more than technical study.

The exercises I use cannot help but keep any voice in a healthier state. Gradually, as the whole range is strengthened through the use of the breath, the "pop" sound will improve in quality and the excessive use of the chesty belt sound will soften and blend into the higher range without the obvious "flip" into what is called "head voice."

I have addressed my remarks mostly to the female voice since the male pop voice is usually a baritone and sings in the chest resonance. The tenor is associated with the female voice because of his higher range.

Certainly the style of pop singers is vastly different from those in the classical field, but it has been proven that in the case of damaged voices, with nodes or polyps developing due to a wrong use of the voice, that the rehabilitation and restoration of the instrument benefits greatly from the classical approach.

Releasing Your Creativity

In the previous chapter I discussed how to discover your voice by learning to listen to your voice, and by listening to other singers. But how do you *free yourself* to become the type of singer you want to be; how do you free yourself to sing the role you want to sing? How do you gain the easy courage of the high diver? We are all taught at a very early age, in varying degrees, not to venture out too far lest we get hurt—or punished! This is essentially what the singer has to unlearn to be free. This is done by forgetting about mechanics, and instead just expressing the music.

Sir Charles Santley is among many masters who observed that focusing on the mechanics of the voice can be a great hindrance to a singer:

> Manuel Garcia is held up as the pioneer of scientific teach-ers of singing. He was—but he taught singing, not surgery! I was a pupil of his in 1858 and a friend of his while he lived, and in all the conversations I had with him, I never heard him say a word about larynx, pharynx, glottis, or any other organ used in the production and emission of the voice. He was perfectly acquainted with their functions, but he used his knowledge for his own direction, not to make a pa-rade of it before his pupils, as he knew it would only serve

to mystify them, and could serve no purpose in acquiring a knowledge of the art of singing. My experience tells me that the less pupils know about the construction of the vocal organs the better; in fact, as I heard a master once remark, "better they should not be aware they had throats except for the purpose of swallowing their food."*

With this in mind, I want to alert you to a number of myths that pervade the singing community. Be aware of these falsehoods—they can hurt your voice and your career.

Ten Myths About the Art of Singing

The following myths are unfortunately all too often accepted as valid theories about singing and study:

MYTH 1: The beauty of the voice depends on consciously controlling muscles.

If this were true, all we would need is a schematic of the muscles and how to manipulate them. To me, this seems at odds with the voice, which is dependent on the ear for discernment.

MYTH 2: The big sound is equivalent to how much space we attempt to make by "opening the throat."

Any conscious attempt to open the throat sends the sound back in the throat and gives a false sense of bigness, which is ONLY heard by the singer. It is a result of tongue pressure and not tone.

MYTH 3: The soft palate must be "consciously" lifted.

This makes for a veiled sound and natural brilliance on high notes becomes impossible.

MYTH: An ill-founded belief held uncritically, especially by an interested group.

MYTHICAL: Fabricated, invented, or imagined in an arbitrary way or in defiance of facts.

SYNONYM: Fictitious

Definitions from Webster's Dictionary

---

* Sir Charles Santley, *The Art of Singing* (The Macmillan Co., 1908)

MYTH 4: *The larynx should be held in a low position.*

"Held" is the key here. In later years, the voice will develop a wobble!

MYTH 5: *Good pronunciation is dependent on knowing where the tongue should be on each vowel setting.*

It is impossible to sing naturally while controlling the muscles in order to enunciate clearly. This practice directs the mind away from the real work—hearing.

MYTH 6: *To the ear of the singer the voice should feel the same size all the way up and down the scale.*

Wrong! Any attempt to make the voice sound and feel the same size on high notes will cause spreading of the sound. The correct solution is allowing the sensation that the voice is smaller, more slender, and with rounded vowels on the top of it. This is clarified elsewhere in the book. The reduction in the length of the cord can then take place naturally. This ensures an easy ascent to the higher voice.

MYTH 7: *The consonant and the vowel are initiated in the same action or place.*

The result makes it seem so, but in reality, the consonant should be felt and take place as if on top of the vowel. The mere whispering of the consonant and then immediately singing the vowel will illustrate this.

MYTH 8: *Greater expulsion of breath gives power to high notes.*

The truth is diametrically opposite. Less breath gives higher intensity. This must be coupled with slender, "non-spacing" in the throat.

MYTH 9: Concentrate only on music and technique in the studio, and then put in the feeling and the characterization when you are onstage.

Every sound you sing, even in rehearsal, must give life to the emotions behind the words. Otherwise, your role will never come to life onstage.

MYTH 10: Wait for contracts before studying roles.

It takes time for the voice to settle into a new role and the discipline of working is hard to recover if you are not in vocal form, or *allenamento* as they say in Italy. Experiment with a role that you know will be in your vocal future. It will help you grow.

Thus we unlearn bad habits as a first step in freeing ourselves. Now that we have peeled away all the outer layers, we can finally get to the core of our creative selves. So let's again address the question, in a slightly different form: How do you create, in yourself, the type of singer you want to be?

Finding the answer to this question has taken me years of study of some of the greatist artists of all types. It is not surprising that the best answers have come from one of the greatest creators of them all, Leonardo da Vinci. I am particulary indebted to Michael Gelb for his brilliant book, *How To Think Like Leonardo da Vinci,** a stunning account of how the master arrived at his outstanding achievements in many artistic endeavors. It is filled with challenging exercises that stretch the mind, imagery, and imagination. This research inspired me to apply Da Vinci's principles to the art of singing. They seem to fit perfectly. The principles are *Curiosità, Dimostrazione, Sensazione, Sfumato, Arte/Scienza, Corporalità,* and *Connessione.*

The natural school...
"As I have said, the natural school... like that of the Italians... stuffed as it is with glorious red blood instead of the white bones of technique (in the misunderstood sense) was the only possible school for me.

Mary Garden –
Great Singers on the Art of Singing, by J.F. Cooke

---

* Michael Gelb, *How To Think Like Leonardo da Vinci* (New York: Dell Publishing, 1998)

Correlation of the Seven Principles of the Art of Leonardo Da Vinci to Singing

Curiosità

Curiosità literally means "curiosity." It is a quest for learning. Mme. Nikolaidi's thinking was the personification of this quality. Words fascinated Nicky. She was vitally interested in history, style, and tradition. Although she was visually impaired at the end of her life, she was constantly aware and curious about everything. She was always humming little phrases, examining their value in teaching. As my friend Jean Houston says, "These are the 'hooks and eyes' that enable us to expand as human beings."

How can you be a colorful performer without curiosity about your music and the composer's intentions? And, how can you improve your sound if you are unwilling to make your vocalises and studies as interesting as your score? These studies translate into communicative performances.

One day in my home, Mme. Nicky heard five of my singers. Her energy was amazing and her childlike simplicity was what made her so unique. I saw each singer begin to express the *music* and not vocal technique. They became compelling in their sounds and their artistry took over. Nicky was full of suggestions about improvising playful ways to approach the music. One of her suggestions was that, to keep from overstating the original content of the text, one could give new meaning to it instead of using the composer's original idea. These things, she said, helped to give the singing more colors. She termed the approach "polychromatic rather than monochromatic." She also advised whispering the words first to make them easier when they were sung. She spoke of *sighing* with breath into the first notes of a phrase rather than *attacking* the sound.

I listen to my body, my muscles, in order to find the right way to the 'armonia' of my face, my body, and my voice. You know, a teacher can say, "Okay, this is a good note, it's fantastic," but if I feel something is not comfortable, I say "I must find the same sound, but easier (laughs). And I've worked very hard.

Mirella Freni –
Interview, *Opera Monthly*

Dimostrazione

The second principle of Leonardo is *Dimostrazione*—that is, demonstration. It really means the ability to evaluate and assess your true potential.

How does this principle apply to your singing? You have compiled many beliefs about your voice, your ability, and your prospects for reaching your goals. Are you easily swayed by the opinions of others about your voice? Can you perform under less than ideal circumstances? Are you constantly criticizing your best efforts even if you do not always come up to your expectations? Are you aware that in looking back you cannot be in the present moment of focus in your singing? The often quoted key is true about singing. BE HERE NOW!

It is helpful and interesting to write a list of your vocal assets. Evaluate what you feel is your true potential. What do you need to do to maximize your possibilities? Who or what have been you greatest influences? (Not only your singing teachers.) Are you expanding your ideas about communicating music? Are you willing to acknowledge to yourself that you need to take "risks" to improve your voice? When you have a new realization about your singing, *test it*! This is true demonstration.

Sensazione

The third principle is *Sensazione*. This refers to the senses and how they affect you. They are, of course, vision, hearing, smell, taste, and touch. The more you develop these senses, the more variety and color your voice will express. Can you sense color through vision? How about your hearing? Is it acute in that you perceive more depth and pleasure from what you hear? Does your sense of smell call forth memories of your childhood and the delights of your mother's cooking? What about

Tetrazzini? What a voice! It does not get down into your heart and thrill you with all sorts of passions and emotions. It does not suggest hours of hard work and evenings of uncertainties. It is like waking in the morning and listening to the voice of a great confident songster.

Geraldine Farrar (speaking about Luisa Tetrazzini) – from *Great Singers on the Art of Singing*, by James Cooke

the smell of freshly cut grass? When you hear a symphony, for instance, the Vivaldi FOUR SEASONS, do you have visual impressions?

Taste and touch play a big part in your use of language. If you experiment with words, you will almost feel how you can touch your emotions through "feelings" and "touching" the inner meaning of the texts.

Cultivate much more awareness of each of the senses and you will experience more dimension in your singing. You will be able to *dimostrare*…demonstrate more emotion than you may have experienced before. The vision of who you are and what you can achieve will expand.

Sfumato

The fourth principle, *Sfumato*, literally means "going up in smoke." Gelb describes it as a willingness to embrace Ambiguity, Paradox, and Uncertainty. Being willing to be open to change, risk, and uncertainty is of primary importance in developing your full potential. Once you have studied your role or song, including coaching it and working out the vocal aspects, you can begin to release the sense of preparation and turn it over to your creative mind to bring out the real meaning of the emotions and feelings behind the text and the music. *This* is where your vocal teacher and your coach must back away and allow you to find yourself in the work. It is a time when you must dare to experiment with your character, visualize him or her in the way you look and move. What are, for you, the main sections that best show your character? How do you relate to the words spoken (sung) to you?

Once you have mentally sketched out your interpretation of your role, you must also realize that you will be asked to follow the staging and tempos of your directors. How you are able to live with the changes and the ambiguity in these situations determines whether you are able to maintain your creative evaluations while being given contradictory or conflicting opinions. Here is the real test for the singer. It is being able to function even with anxiety, ambiguity, and directions that seem to limit your freedom in the work. Here it is good to summon up a quality that we have already addressed: *curiosità*, or curiosity. It is accepting the unknown, the uncertainty, and finding your meaning within it.

The Scottish poet Robert Burns once penned the famous line, "Best laid plans o' mice an' men gang aft agley," meaning, "the best laid plans often go awry." If you can live with this truth and appreciate its greater importance, you will have understood the true meaning of *sfumato*.

The mind paints before the brush.
James Ellis – *The Art of Painting*

Arte/Scienza

The next principle is *Arte/Scienza*. Gelb describes this as "the development of the balance between Science, Art, Logic, and Imagination." That is, *whole brain* thinking.

Nobel Prize winner Professor Roger Sperry found that in most cases the left hemisphere of the brain is responsible for analytical thinking while the right hemisphere is the creative, imaginative side of the brain. (It is also interesting to note that left-handed people are considered mostly "right-brain" thinkers.) Da Vinci had the amazing ability to excel in his studies of science and "translate" them into expressive works of art.

How can the concept of *Arte/Scienza* help you in your singing? One of the main characteristics of a beautiful voice is one that is equal throughout its entire range. Vocal study is aimed at achieving this result. The sense of *balance* in the sound as well as the expression of the music is all a part of effective performance.

I do not believe any of us are exclusively "left brained" or "right brained" in our makeup, but it is interesting to ponder a few of the qualities of each as they apply to singing and the necessary preparation for performance.

The left-brained person is, by nature, said to be more orderly about details. He or she is more analytical, articulate, and organized. In themselves, these are very important qualities in the study of language, scores, and stage techniques. This was the manner of preparation Leonardo used in his scientific studies. Once completed, however, he put those aside and allowed himself to use imagery, intuition, and his remarkable imagination before he sketched or painted. This faculty is the "right-brain" activity. In singing, it involves the necessity to trust, the excitement of creating something new, and the spontaneous use of the voice, all of which bring music to life.

As singers, we must do the analytical steps of preparation that are necessary to finally allow us the freedom to explore the "big picture" while performing. My hope in teaching is to simplify the approach to a few basic concepts and, through the education of the singer's ear, to bring him to a place where the action of the voice becomes involuntary and simply carries out the "mental" desire of the singer. It involves repetition, an unhurried manner of working, and the search for a "childlike" spontaneity without fear of failure.

In concluding the idea of this principle, I want to add a comment about two interesting statements made by the distinguished baritone, Thomas Allen, taken from a short television program on the Bravo channel, called "Aria and Pasta." In speaking about his career and preparation of roles, Allen singled out DON GIOVANNI as his favorite. He said that through his study of the role, history, and the background of the work he felt a strong kinship with the character. However, on being questioned on how his interpretation had changed with time, he replied, "I start with a completely clean slate every time I sing the role." He went on to say that he allows himself to rely on the inspiration of the moment. This can only evolve from the initial preparation done with the faculties of the "left brain." The freedom to create "anew" comes from the studies prior to the performance mode. Then the "right brain" takes over and is free to express spontaneously.

Corporalità

The sixth principle from Leonardo is *corporalità*. Da Vinci thought that we should accept the responsibility for our health and well-being. He viewed sickness as the discord of the effects of destructive attitudes and emotions. Have you ever experienced how a particular event or negative emotions produced a cold, or the inability to concentrate, or to sing something you found easy before? The body/mind coordination is linked to your state of mind.

As a singer, your voice, mind, and body must be thought of as a complete unity. If you experience difficulty in a phrase or a particular note, stop and assess where you feel tension or are out of balance. Is your head tilting to the side? Do you know what happens to your awareness and sensory perception if your head is not properly aligned at the top of your spine? I often say that you should feel as if your head is being drawn upward gently as you stand. This aids in better alignment overall.

See yourself as moving effortlessly as a dancer, and your voice should feel as if it comes from being centered in your body and not in your throat or neck. I am not of the school that believes you must stand motionless and constrained in order to sing well. You should feel and react to the rhythm, tempo, and meaning of the text. Each character you interpret in an opera has posture that must enhance the personage. For example, how does the walk of Aïda differ from that of Amneris, although both are royal in their own societies? How does the body movement of Scarpia differ from that of Germont?

The costumes and historical backgrounds have much to do with movement as well. I was amazed at how different and *ineffective* the entrance of Tosca was in a performance staged in the period of the 1950s—namely, to see Eva Marton in flat shoes and wearing a pageboy hairdo! The younger stage directors are attempting to update opera to appeal to a new audience. Time will also tell if staging Bach cantatas is more effective than in concert performance.

Connessione

The final principle of Leonardo's creed is that of *Connessione*, meaning "connection." It applies in many ways to the work of the singer. It can mean the connection between the breath and the sound, as well as the meaningful connection of the singer to the music. Another aspect of the singer's art is the connection of feelings in the sound that he sings. The dynamics of music depend on the ebb and flow of feelings as they course through the sounds. This is the key to communication. It lifts vocal technique to another level of mastery.

Try living a day with the "knowing" that all events are connected and that there is something you can apply to your singing, whether it is a need for patience, compassion, self-acceptance, or a new idea for study. Keep your work fresh by expanding your interest in other arts—sculpture, painting, and dance of all kinds. It will open you to the bigger picture of man's feeling about art.

To finalize this section of study, I want to add a quotation from Gelb's book. It is taken from Serge Bramly on Leonardo's spirituality:

> He discovered...God in the miraculous beauty of light, in the harmonious movement of the planets, in the intricate arrangement of muscles and nerves inside the human body, and in that inexpressible masterpiece, the human soul.

Part 3

A Collection of Rare and
Original Vocalises

ESTETICA | ESTHETIQUE | ESTHETICS

DEL | DU | OF THE ART OF

CANTO | CHANT | SINGING

E DELL'ARTE | ET DE | AND OF THE

Melodrammatica | L'Art Lyrique | Melodrama

Introduction to the Vocalises

This section of the book contains the rarest of materials I have collected over many years. I attribute my keen interest and curiosity about the school of bel canto to my first teacher, Lena Kershner. Later, when I began to study in Paris, I searched in all the old, rare bookstores, as well as the *bouquinistes*, the open bookstalls all along the Seine. My teacher in Paris, Maria Castellazzi-Bovy, had sung for years at La Scala and often spoke to me about her many experiences with teachers in Italy in the early 1900s. Above all, she impressed me with the ideals of beautiful singing and the serious studies followed by the singers of the past. Her maestro was from the school of Brambilla. You will find in this section some of the Brambilla vocalises I studied.

You will also find vocalises of Rubini and Lablache, two of the most famous singers when the music of Rossini, Donizetti, and Bellini was being written. Other materials of interest included are the exercises of the fabled soprano Adelina Patti, often regarded as a perfect singer. Lilli Lehmann needs no introduction, for her book on singing is well known,* but the work of Clara Doria is not generally known and, for me, it is perhaps some of the more valuable of all the material.

* Lilli Lehmann, *How to Sing* (New York: The MacMillan Co., 1929).

Both Clara Doria and Delle Sedie give very clear graphs on vowel modification, a foundation I have come to use in my teaching.

I have also included the original page from my notebook when I studied with Rosa Ponselle. It was written for me by her accompanist. It is a treasure I want to share with you.

My own vocalises have been collected and written to clarify the principles I teach. They show the principles in action. I constantly discover new ones, but what you have here are the ones I use most frequently. The approach is to acquire evenness in the movement from one vowel to another, to lead the student to be aware of his best sounds, and to eliminate the sense of having to "place" every note. All sounds should seem to originate from one centered place. Experiment with the vowel modification. You will recognize when the sounds become easier. The voice will then become centered and unified throughout its range.

The Brambilla exercises on *legato* and the study of the *cadenza* are very important for the singer who has advanced sufficiently to master them. The vocalises and charts are merely guides to awaken your curiosity about what the early masters taught. They must be studied and put into practice only when they make sense to *you*.

As a final word about vocalizing, I urge you to put into it the same emotion, intensity, and imagery that you use when singing an aria. Delle Sedie has a whole treatise on the importance of meaning in vocalizing. In it he does many things to evoke feelings—he even puts quotes of great poetry beside the music to stretch the singer's creativity, or tells the singer what shade of emotion is required.

I suggest that you allow at least twenty minutes for these vocalises, and take a rest before proceeding on to your music. And most importantly, when you feel fatigue or diminished concentration, rest before continuing.

The Scale and Passaggi

The ideal scale is one that has a homogenous sound throughout. The following are the two most important studies to accomplish this:

1. Understanding how close the vowels are to each other. Acquiring this skill entails the conscious training of the ear.

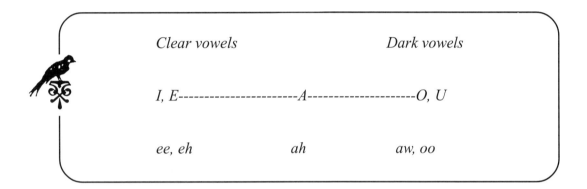

Clear vowels   *Dark vowels*

I, E----------------------A--------------------O, U

ee, eh   *ah*   *aw, oo*

It is helpful to think of the light vowels as a bit darker or rounder and the darker vowels as lighter. The A is the center area between them.

2. Paying careful attention to reducing or rounding the vowels in the *passaggio*. By "reducing" I mean "conceiving" the size of the vowel as being smaller, not larger, as you proceed higher in the range. This eliminates the idea of spreading the tone and keeps the scale even.

Zones of the Passaggio

The following graph on the zones of the *passaggio* is not a rule for all voices because all voices are different. These are only guidelines. It is helpful to think of the voice, when singing in this area, as more compact, with the vowels intentionally rounded. Singing the word "bird," the basic sound being "buh" and a disappearing "R", is a good way to feel the closeness of the pitches in those areas. (Refer to the chapter on Registers.)

Here are the generally accepted zones of the *passaggio* in each voice; they are copies of the original Lablache materials:

TENOR AND SOPRANO

MEZZO-SOPRANO

BARITONE

CONTRALTO

BASS

Voice Ranges for Transposing

Before beginning the vocalises, look at the below graph (a copy of the original Lablache) showing the ranges in which they must be transposed. It is best to proceed by semi-tones ascending and descending. Above all, do not push for the extremes of your range.

Lois Alba as the Marschallin in DER ROSENKAVALIER. Costume is
Lotte Lehmann's, which she wore at the Vienna Staatsoper.

Vocalises of Lois Alba

Here are the basic exercises I use for "warming up" the voice. Remember that vocalizing should be the gradual "warming" of the voice, not a frenetic race to get to fast scales and the extremes of the range.

First, some general comments:

1. The throat should be still when the breath is taken.

2. There should be a gradual expansion of the diaphragm as the lungs fill. Expansion can be felt at the waist as well as in the back. There should be no conscious attempt to expand the diaphragm.

3. The initiation of the sound is a result of the clear intention to execute the pitch and the vowel.

4. The humming is merely to feel the sound in the chest as well as the head.

5. The appoggio, or leaning into the sound, comes as a result of the release of the air to the sound intended.

The first track of the enclosed CD contains further instructions, and the music, for each of these twelve vocalises.

Vocalise One: Humming Exercise

Gently hum this with the mouth slightly closed. Be careful not to clench the teeth or the jaw. Think of the word MAW while humming. The face will appear long.

Vocalise Two: The Vowels

The next is a sequence of vowels, and the idea is to feel the close proximity of each to the next. The eh sound must be an open eh and the ee is close to the sound as pronounced in the word "wheat."

Vocalise Three: Droning, for Smoothness

This must be sung smoothly, thinking of DRONING, as explained in the text.

Vocalise Four: A Study in Triplets, for Elasticity

This is a study in triplets to give the voice elasticity. It must be performed smoothly and with a minimal movement of the mouth in its execution.

Vocalise Five: Ponselle's "Moo" Exercise

Ponselle used this exercise to "warm up." The original, written for me by her accompanist, follows my vocalises.

Vocalise Six: For Legato and Staccato

This must be sung as if on one level, not reaching. The first repetition is *legato*, and the second is *staccato* on the last four notes.

Vocalise Seven: The Rabbit Jumping Exercise

I call this my rabbit jumping exercise! (I think we need a bit of humor in this serious business of vocalises.) It sounds a bit like hopping, but there should be no sensation of control in the throat. The control comes from the action of the diaphragm as a result of the intention to sing the exercise. This is for sopranos, and helps extend their range. It could be used by a light tenor, but not a *spinto*.

Vocalise Eight: For Developing Legato in Scales

This is a scale sung with the designated sequence of vowels. Smoothness is the key here. It is very fine for developing a good *legato* in scale work. The feeling is as if you are singing in a horizontal direction, not that of climbing. If anything, the lower note should be perceived as the higher one, and as the scale goes higher, the notes should feel slightly lower.

Vocalise Nine: Ponselle's Exercise with Italian Words

The following exercise uses all the Italian vowels in words. It is another of Ponselle's vocalises that you will find on the original page of my notebook when I studied with her.

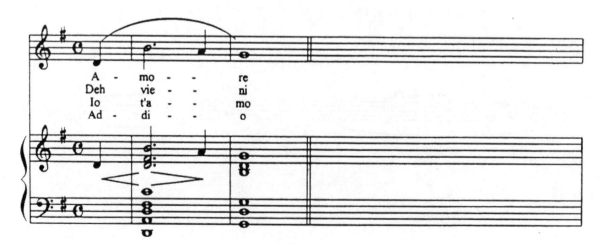

Vocalise Ten: For Equalizing the Voice Throughout the Range

This is a good study for equalizing the voice throughout the range. It is particularly good for the tenor voice. The sensation is one of droning, and the higher you sing, the more it is felt to be descending. I learned this exercise from a wonderful tenor, Govanni Consiglio. He was able to sing with ease to a high C.

Vocalise Eleven: For Feeling the Voice as a Whole

I developed this exercise to help the singer feel the voice as a whole, in whatever range. Of course, vowel modification applies here as well.

Vocalise Twelve: A Great Equalizer

This exercise was given to me by a very fine tenor of the "old school." It is also a great equalizer and uses vowel modification as it ascends.

Original Exercise from Rosa Ponselle

This is the original page from my notebook when I studied with Rosa Ponselle. Her exercises were written for me by her accompanist.

On the Study of Cadenzas

The study of passages can be simplified if they are divided into sections and practiced slowly. Below are two examples from an aria in DINORAH. When practiced in this manner, the ear quickly memorizes the notes and they will flow easily.

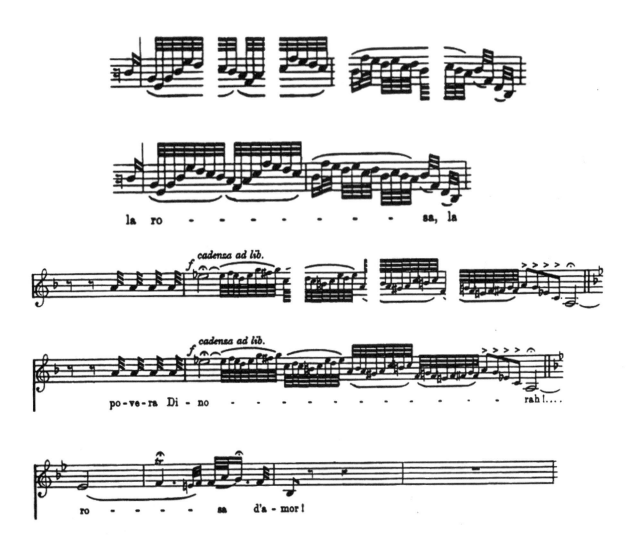

A final note: It is best to diminish the note leading into any florid passage. This ensures the release of the breath, and the passage becomes more fluid and clear in its execution.

Portamento

Portamento literally means "carrying" the sound. In the case of descent from a higher pitch to a lower one, as shown in the example, you descend lightly in a *decrescendo*, adding a small grace note before singing the following word.

In the aria "Mi Chiamano Mimì," the passage in the first phrase has two marked *portamenti*. These are Puccini's indications. The way to make them expressive is to make a slight *decrescendo* on the "no" in "chiamano" in order to arrive gracefully on the E-natural, and add a little accent on the last "mi" in "Mimi."

A Well Known Vocalise

Here is a well known vocalise that has been used by many great singers. The first measure is sung on <u>ee</u>, and the second on <u>ah</u> (slightly rounded toward <u>aw</u>), returning to the <u>ee</u> again on the last two measures. This is attributed to Caruso, but many singers claim to have written it.

DOUZE LEÇONS

DE CHANT MODERNE

Pour voix de Ténor ou Soprano

par

RUBINI

Du Théâtre Italien de Paris.

Dédiées à son ami le Maestro URANIO FONTANA

Nº 5514. —— Propriété des Editeurs —— Pr. 20

Enrégistré aux Archives de l'union

MAYENCE et ANVERS

Chez les fils de B. Schott.

à Paris, chez Bernard Latte   à Londres, chez Cramer, Addison & Cie

Dépôt général de notre fonds de Musique

à Leipzig, chez G.me Haertel.   à Vienne, chez H. F. Müller.

Vocalises of Giovanni Battista Rubini (1794-1854)

Rubini was the tenor for whom Bellini composed many of his operas. They were BIANCA E GERNANDO in 1826 (Naples), IL PIRATA in 1835 (Paris), LA SONNAMBULA in 1831 (Milan), and I PURITANI in 1835 (Paris). Rubini's phenomenal range inspired Bellini to include a high F in the third act of I PURITANI. Rubini is also credited with introducing the Romantic mannerism…the sob.

I have included an example of a vocalise from Rubini's book, *Douze Lecons de Chant Moderne pour voix de Ténor ou Soprano*, published in Paris and London, circa 1830.

For Even and Sustained Notes and Portamento

MÉTHODE

complète

DE CHANT

OU

*Analyse raisonnée des Principes d'après lesquels
on doit diriger les Études pour développer la Voix,
la rendre légère et pour former le goût*

avec

EXEMPLES DÉMONSTRATIFS, EXERCICES ET VOCALISES GRADUÉES

PAR

LOUIS LABLACHE

PREMIER CHANTEUR

de la Chambre & *de la Chapelle*

DE

S. M.

le Roi des Deux-Siciles

Prix   30 f

J. Derhayer Sculp.ᵗ 1840.

Vocalises of Luigi Lablache (1794-1858)

The Italian bass Luigi Lablache created many of the leading roles in Bellini's operas, and sang the first performance of Georgio in I PURITANI with Giulia Grisi and the tenor, Rubini.

The Divisions of the Voice

This is a chart on the divisions of the voice, with textural passages following, given in Lablache's book, *Méthode Completè*, published in Paris by Les Fils de B. Schotte, circa 1830.

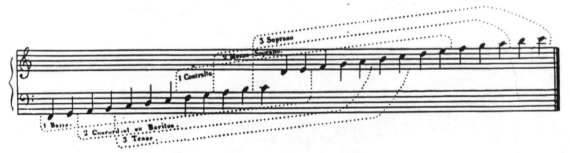

"This is an example showing the six types of voices, the bass, the baritone, and the tenor, as well as the three voices of women, the contralto, the mezzo-soprano, and the soprano. You will observe the numbers 1, 2, and 3 in the voices of the women correspond to the same numbers in the men's voices, an octave lower. The contralto has the same extension as the bass."

The Registers of the Voice

Free translation:

"Men have the ability to form two series of sounds that are called the registers of the chest and the head. The first begins with the lowest notes and extends to E above the staff in the bass clef. Above these is the second series, called the head. The true bass voice has very little possibility to use the head voice.

The baritone and the tenor voices are less dense, sweeter, and more flexible. They can make use of the two registers in the following manner.

The voice of the woman is divided into three series of sounds (registers). They are chest, medium, and head. Like the bass, the contralto rarely uses the head register."

Following is the chart showing the divisions of the so-called registers:

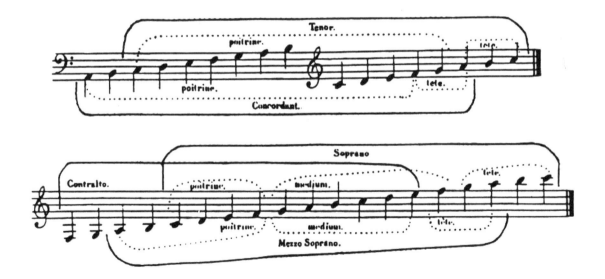

A Study of Cadenzas

Free translation:

"The *cadenza* is dependent on the ability and the good taste of the executants. It is necessary to make the student aware of certain abuses in execution. Above all, the composer's composition should dictate the style and character of the *cadenza*. Furthermore, it can be out of place in music expressing the highest passion, and should not be inserted for the sole purpose of showing off the agility and range of the voice. It is important to conserve the breath carefully in order not to arrive tired at the end, destroying all the effect."

The following are different examples that the student will encounter. (I suggest you observe the accents and the markings on each one.) These *cadenzas* can, of course, be transposed for lower voices.

NEUNTE LEKTION.

CADENZ, SCHLUSSFALL.

Die Cadenz, welche der Fähigkeit und dem guten Geschmack des Ausführenden gänzlich überlassen ist, kann auf sehr verschiedene Weise ausgeführt werden. Nöthig erscheint es daher, den Schüler auf den Missbrauch derselben aufmerksam zu machen.

Die Verzierungen, welche man sowohl bei der Cadenz als auch im Verlauf eines Musikstückes anbringt, dürfen sich nie von dem Charakter entfernen welchen der Autor seiner Composition hat geben wollen. Bei einem Musikstücke, worin der höchste Grad der Leidenschafft ausgedrückt, oder bei einem solchen, worin der Ausdruck zarter Melancholie vorherschend ist, würde es daher sehr am unrechten Orte sein mit seinen Gesangmitteln glänzen zu wollen; auf wenige bedeutungsvolle und dem Charakter der Composition entsprechende Noten muss man sich in solchen Fällen beschränken. Auch muss man sehr darauf bedacht sein, für die letzten Noten der Cadenz den Athem, soviel es nur immerhin möglich ist, aufzubewahren, denn der Sänger, welcher bei dem Ende erschöpft ankömmt, wird nicht allein alle Wirkung der Cadenz verfehlen sondern auch noch der vorhergehenden Ausführung Schaden bringen.

Im Laufe dieser Lektionen wird der Schüler zwar schon verschiedene Beispiele der Cadenzen gefunden haben; um das eben gesagte aber besser würdigen zu lernen mögen hierbei noch einige andere folgen.

EINFACHE CADENZ.

Um mit Kraft zu endigen.

LEÇON 9me.

DU POINT D'ORGUE.

Le Point d'orgue est susceptible des interpretations les plus variées étant soumis entièrement aux facultés et au bon gout des exécutans. Il est nécessaire pourtant de prévenir l'élève de l'abus qu'on en peut faire.

Les agréments que l'on introduit dans le point d'orgue comme dans le courant du morceau ne doivent pas s'éloigner du caractère que l'auteur a voulu donner à sa composition. Ainsi il serait très déplacé dans un morceau ou la passion est exprimée à son plus haut dégré comme dans ceux ou domine une tendre mélancolie de saisir l'instant du point d'orgue pour faire parade de ses moyens de vocalisation; on devra se limiter à peu de notes bien nuancées et en rapport avec le caractère de la composition. Il faut aussi avoir bien soin de conserver pour les dernières notes du point d'orgue la plus grande quantité de respiration possible, car si le chanteur arrivait à la fin épuisé, l'effet en serait entièrement manqué et nuirait aussi à l'exécution antérieure.

Dans le courant de ces leçons l'élève aura déja rencontré différents exemples de Point d'orgue: nous allons encore en donner quelques uns pour mieux faire apprécier ce que nous venons de dire.

POINT D'ORGUE SIMPLE.

Pour finir avec force.

Exemples Démonstratifs

The following is an exciting example of how to do ornamentation. First is a shortened translation of Lablache's description:

"There are two rules that are dictated by good taste, and they must not be disregarded when ornamenting the melody:

1. They must not obliterate nor change the phrase,

2. The ornaments must always be in keeping with the character of the piece.

Here are a few simple phrases with ornamentation which, by the variety of color, may be applied to melodies of varying character (light; tender; passionate; brilliant; elegant; graceful; sad; fiery)."

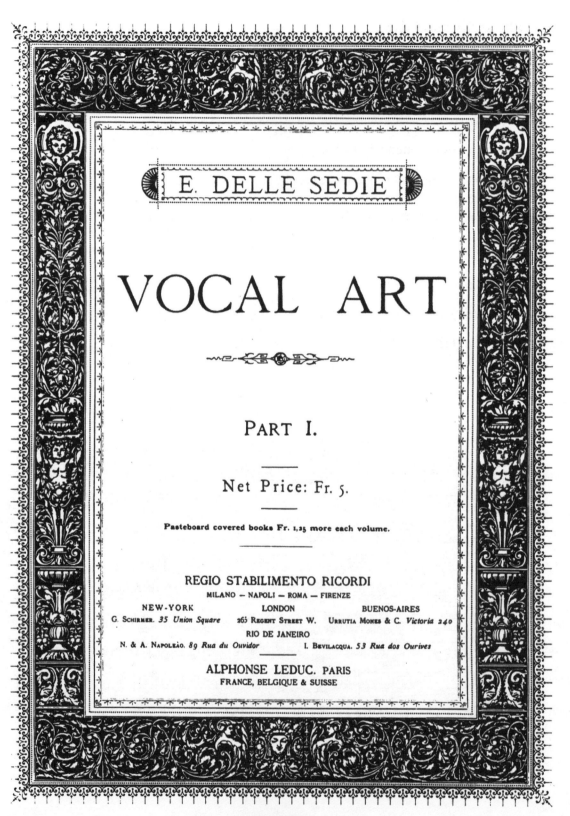

E. DELLE SEDIE

VOCAL ART

PART I.

Net Price: Fr. 5.

Pasteboard covered books Fr. 1,25 more each volume.

REGIO STABILIMENTO RICORDI
MILANO — NAPOLI — ROMA — FIRENZE

NEW-YORK   LONDON   BUENOS-AIRES

G. Schirmer. *35 Union Square*   265 Regent Street W.   Urrutia Mones & C. *Victoria 240*

RIO DE JANEIRO

N. & A. Napoleào. *89 Rua du Ouvidor*   I. Bevilacqua. *53 Rua dos Ourives*

ALPHONSE LEDUC. PARIS
FRANCE, BELGIQUE & SUISSE

Vocalises of Enrico Delle Sedie (1822-1907)

Delle Sedie was a baritone who studied with Carlo Galeffi. He taught at the Paris Conservatoire from 1876 to 1886, and wrote a book in 1881 on the decline of the Italian School of Singing, entitled *Reflessioni sulle Cause della decadenza della Scuola di Canto in Italia* (Reflections on the decline of the School of Singing in Italy).

The Phonic Shades Inherent to the Vocal Scale

TAVOLA COMPARATIVA DELLE GRADAZIONI FONICHE INERENTI ALLA SCALA VOCALE	TABLE COMPARATIVE DES NUANCES PHONIQUES INHERENTES A LA GAMME VOCALE	COMPARATIVE TABLE OF THE PHONICAL SHADES INHERENT TO THE VOCAL SCALE
La parola posta contro la nota musicale serve per indicare l'accento fonico della vocale corrispondente al suono di quella nota. Questa vocale è messa in evidenza per mezzo di segni speciali apposti alla vocale citata.	Les mots mis en regard des notes servent à indiquer l'accent phonique de la voyelle correspondant au son vocal, et celle-ci est signalée par des lignes spéciales posées auprès de la voyelle même.	The words placed at the sides of the notes serve to show us that the phonic accent of the vowel corresponding to the vocal sound, is marked by special lines and placed after the same vowel.
ā aperta come nel la parola Bāndo	à ouvert comme dans l'ā de Climāt	ā open as in the word..... Bār
a semioscura come nella parola Bautta	a un peu sombre comme dans l'a de Courage	a a little closed as in the word.: Father
ā oscura come nel la parola Fārmaco	ā sombre comme dans l'ā de Caprice	ā closed as in the word...... Cāto
â grave come nel la parola Gâudio	â grave comme dans l'â de Grâce	â grave as in the word ..... Wâs
ā aperta come nel la parola Bāndo	ā ouvert comme dans l'ā de Climāt	ā open as in the word...... Bār
â grave come nel la parola Gâudio	â grave comme dans l'â de Grâce	â grave as in the word ..... Wâs
ō chiusa come nel la parola Dólce	ō fermé comme dans l'ō de Idōle	ō closed as in the word...... Ōr
ô grave come nel la parola Dôlo	ô grave comme dans l'ô de Pôle	ô grave as in the word...... Pôle
eū chiuso come nel la parola francese Jeūne	eū fermé comme l'eū dans Jeūne	eū closed as in the french word .. Jeūne
eu grave come nel la parola francese Feu	eu grave comme l'eu dans Feu	eu grave as in the french word . Feu
ē muta come nella parola francese Naturē	ē muet comme l'ē dans Naturē	ē mute as in the word..... Naturē
e muta oscura come nella par. fr. Refrain	e muet couvert comme dans l'e de Refrain	e mute covered as in the word. Her

Blending of the Registers: 1st Part of the Decrescendo

BLENDING OF THE REGISTERS

I" PART

OF THE DECRESCÈNDO

We have shown in the preliminaries that each isolated sound is a vowel and that its timbre varies according to the number and intensity of the harmonics it contains, so we may admit that the sounds of the human voice are subject to the laws of harmonics ([1]) the character of the fundamental note depends on the shape of the mouth and on the pressure of air against the glottis; in the *forte* the fundamental note dominates so much over the other harmonics that they become almost indeterminable to the ear. In the *piano* on the contrary its intensity diminishes and the other harmonics reappear.

As the sound which is the octave of the fundamental note is the most distinct to the ear, it seems that the *decrescendo ascends an octave.* A study based on the *decrescendo* must consequently lead the pupil to make the sounds differently timbred equal.

We must execute the following exercise by attacking the sound as mentioned in the Lesson I, arriving at the resonance of the higher octave by the *decrescendo* only, as the pressure of air is stronger for the *forte*, it must be slightly diminished for the *decrescendo*.

The pupil in emitting the note, may strike it on the piano so that the voice may be guided by the natural effect of the vibration of the chord. In order to facilitate the execution of the *decrescendo* the intermediary vowels are here employed, as is indicated under the first notes of this exercise, to avoid a too notable change in the position of the lips while passing from *A* to *A*, *EU* and *È* and to unite the timbres as much as possible.

(¹) The human voice is generally divided into several series of consecutive sounds, called registers, which are known by their timbre. The great difficulty has always been to blend these registers so there might be no solution of continuity in the timbre. To attain that object, we base this study on the *decrescendo* conserving the registers with the denominations by which they are generally distinguished, in order to make our idea more comprehensible.

DENOMINATION OF THE REGISTERS

1ˢᵗ Cʜᴇsᴛ ᴠoɪᴄᴇ
2 Mᴇᴅɪᴜᴍ ᴠoɪᴄᴇ
3 Hᴇᴀᴅ ᴠoɪᴄᴇ oʀ ꜰᴀʟsᴇᴛᴛo.

We think it is useless to mention their limits, for we wish to blend them progressively by the natural laws of harmonics.

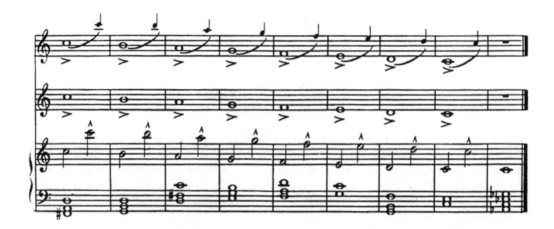

After acquiring a satisfactory execution in every tone by a chromatic progression of the exercise No. 3, we shall pass to the next one being careful to carry the first sound, by *descrescendo*, on to the second which must only be emitted at the end of the pianissimo.

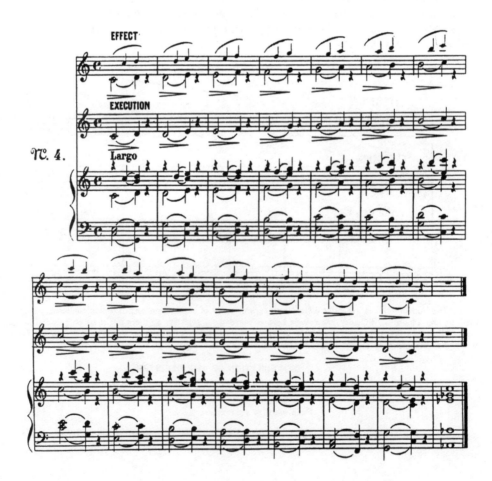

For the following exercise, the same system is to be employed, always conserving the resonance of the higher octave.

The interval of the *second* in this case is produced rather at the higher octave than at that marked by the written musical notes as if the passage were to be executed, with out-the *decrescendo*.

This demonstration is to explain the phenomenon of which we speak; for by this we may effect a *second* by the *decrescendo*, while the effect produced by the displacement of the higher harmonics of the initial sound produces to the ear the sensation of the interval of the *octave* followed by the *ninth*. So its execution is the following:

The same phenomenon takes place in the case of the *decrescendo* for the interval of the third, of the fourth and so on; the effect perceptible to the ear, is that of the *octave*, of the *ninth* and of the *tenth*, for the three notes; as follows:

emitted as if they were written in the following way:

Follow the exercises on two and three notes.

Or donc, l'intervalle de *seconde*, par exemple, se produira dans ce cas, plutôt à l'octave supérieure qu'à celui marqué par les notes musicales écrites, comme si l'on devait exécuter le passage suivant, sans opérer le *decrescendo*.

Cette démonstration est uniquement destinée à expliquer le phénomène dont il s'agit, car par le *decrescendo*, on effectue une *seconde* par *decrescendo*, tandis que l'effet produit par le déplacement des harmoniques élevées du son initial produit à l'oreille la sensation de l'intervalle de l'*octave* suivi de la *neuvième*. Donc, son exécution n'est autre que la suivante:

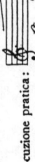

Le même phénomène a lieu, dans le cas du *decrescendo*, pour les intervalles de *tierce*, de *quarte* et ainsi de suite, dont l'effet appréciable à l'oreille est de l'*octave*, de la *neuvième* et de la *dixième*, pour les trois notes, placées comme suit:

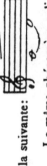

qui s'émettent comme si elles étaient écrites de la manière suivante:

Suivent les exercices sur deux et sur trois notes.

In questo caso, l'intervallo di *seconda* si produrrà piuttosto all'ottava superiore che a quella segnata dalle note musicali scritte, come se si dovesse eseguire il seguente passaggio senza operare il *decrescendo*.

Questa dimostrazione è unicamente destinata a spiegare il fenomeno di cui parliamo, perchè per il *decrescendo* si effettua una *seconda* per *decrescendo*, mentre l'effetto prodotto dallo spostamento degli armonici elevati del suono iniziale produce all'orecchio la sensazione dell'intervallo dell'*ottava* seguita dalla *nona*. La seguente è dunque la sua esecuzione pratica:

Lo stesso fenomeno succede nel caso del *decrescendo* pegli intervalli di *terza*, di *quarta* e successivi, il di cui effetto riesce percettibile all'orecchio; come se apparisse l'*ottava*, la *nona* e la *decima* per le tre note nella posizione seguente:

le quali si emettono come se fossero scritte in questa maniera:

Seguono gli esercizi a due e tre note.

Secondo quello che abbiamo esposto più sopra sullo spostamento degli armonici del suono, il *forte* aggruppando intorno al suono fondamentale tutti gli armonici, provoca un timbro di risonanza grave corrispondente ad un' *A* che partecipa dell' *O* aperta, da potersi comparare approssimativamente all' *A* grave della parola GAUDIO. Cominceremo dunque da questa vocale per effettuare la nostra dimostrazione pratica, che faremo seguire successivamente dalle vocali che comportano delle gradazioni regolari in conformità all' affievolirsi dell' intensità ed alla elevazione della risonanza; in tal modo, giungeremo ad ottenere il *decrescendo* rappresentato dall' *E* muta come nella parola francese REFRAIN. Il suono sul quale si effettua il nostro esperimento sarà rappresentato da una nota del *medium* della voce, il di cui valore è quello di una *breve*, e serve a rappresentare la vocale iniziale. Al rigo superiore saranno poste, corrispondenti alla durata della *breve* tante *semiminime*, le quali serviranno a rappresentare i timbri (vocali) pei quali si effettua il trasmutare dei suoni armonici che nel *forte* si trovano aggruppati intorno alla *tonica*, al disopra di queste *semiminime* saranno poste le vocali conformemente alla tavola comparativa già citata.

Esempio:

D'après ce que nous avons exposé plus haut sur le déplacement des harmoniques du son, le *forte* groupant autour du son fondamental toutes ses harmoniques, provoque un timbre de résonnance grave correspondant à un *A* qui tient de l'*O* ouvert; on peut le comparer approximativement à l'*A* grave de la parole GRACE. Nous partirons donc de cette voyelle pour effectuer notre démonstration pratique; et abordant successivement les voyelles qui comportent des dégradations régulières, en conformité avec l'affaiblissement de l'intensité et l'élévation de la résonnance, nous arriverons à produire le *decrescendo* représenté (comme nous savons) par l'*E* muet comme dans REFRAIN. Le son sur lequel va s'effectuer notre expérience, sera représenté par une note du médium de la voix; sa valeur sera celle d'une *brève*; elle servira à représenter la voyelle initiale. A la portée supérieure seront posées, correspondant à la durée de la *brève* autant de *noires*, qui serviront à représenter les timbres ou voyelles, par lesquels s'effectue le déplacement des sons harmoniques, sons qui dans le *forte* se trouvaient groupés autour de la *tonique*. Au-dessus de ces noires seront posées les voyelles conformes à la table comparative déjà citée

Exemple:

After what we have said on the displacement of the harmonics of sound, the *forte* uniting all its harmonics with the fundamental sound provokes a tone of grave resonance corresponding to an *A*, participating of the open *O* approximatively compared to the *A* grave in the word WAS. We now start from this vowel to effect our practical demonstration, and by going successively through the vowels bearing regular degradations in conformity with the weakness of the intensity and the height of the resonance, we succeed in producing the *decrescendo* represented by the *E* mute as in the word HER.

The sound which will serve for our experiment will be represented by a note from the medium of the voice; its value will be that of a *breve*; and will represent the initial vowel. At the superior stave will be placed, corresponding to the duration of the *breve*, so many *crotchets*, representing the timbre of vowels affecting the displacement of the harmonic sounds, which in the forte are grouped about the *tonic*. Above the crotchets we place the vowels answering to the comparative table already spoken of.

Example:

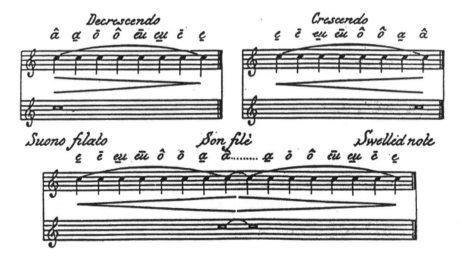

MARIETTA BRAMBILLA

Esercizi e Vocalizzi

PER SOPRANO

con accompagnamento di Pianoforte

19499	Libro I. ESERCIZI	. . . .	(B) L. 7.—
19500	Libro II. VOCALIZZI	. . . .	12.—

G. RICORDI & C.
MILANO
ROMA - NAPOLI - PALERMO
LEIPZIG - BUENOS AIRES - S. PAULO
LONDON: G. RICORDI & Co., (LONDON) LTD.
NEW YORK: G. RICORDI & Co., INC.

(Printed in Italy)   (Imprimé en Italie)

Vocalises of Marietta Brambilla (1807-1875)

The contralto Marietta Brambilla, one of the most important singers of the nineteenth century, came from a family of singers. Donizetti composed two male roles for her, including that of Orsini in LUCREZIA BORGIA in 1883. She established a school of singing which was exemplary of the school of bel canto.

The following vocalises from Brambilla are from her *Esercizi e Vocalizzi per Soprano*. These may be transposed for other voices.

An Exercise on Legato

Here is an exercise from Brambilla meant to promote evenness throughout the entire scale.

This is especially helpful for sopranos and tenors.

A Study on the Singing of Cadenzas

The following is a study on the singing of cadenzas. My teacher added the high C at the end!

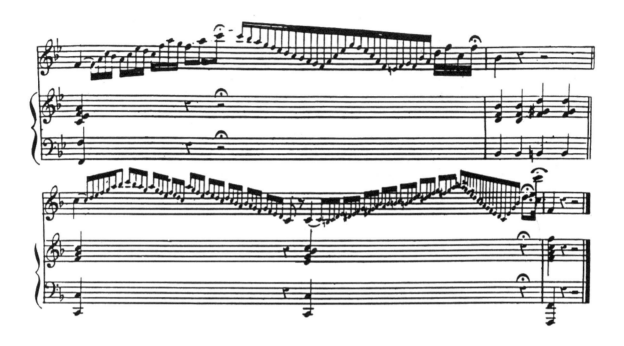

Vocalises of Adelina Patti (1843-1919)

Adelina Patti was an Italian soprano noted for her amazing purity of voice and the vocal flexibility she retained to the end of her career. Her farewell performances were in Covent Garden in 1895. The following exercises are Patti's "Ten Commandments." Notice how similar they are to others I have given you.

The "Ten Commandments" of Adelina Patti

Vocalises of Lilli Lehmann (1848-1929)

The great German soprano, Lilli Lehmann, was a unique singer whose repertoire included both the dramatic coloratura roles as well as Wagner. Lehmann's book, *How To Sing,** is a classic. There were a few recordings made of her singing, done late in her career when she was in her mid-sixties. The "great scale," as she named it, was Lehmann's daily study. She declared it the most important of all, and practiced it daily over a range of two octaves. She said: "I rely absolutely on its assistance. I often take 50 minutes to go through it once, for I let no tone pass that is lacking in any degree in pitch, power, duration, or in any single vibration."

* Lilli Lehmann, *How to Sing* (New York: The MacMillan Co., 1914).

The "Great Scale"

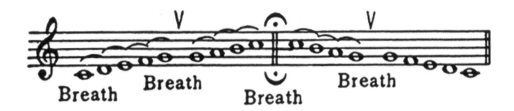

Trill

TRILL

THERE still remains the trill, which is best practised in the beginning as follows—always from the upper note to the lower one:

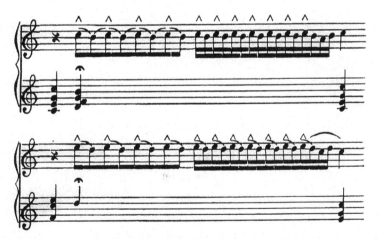

$\bar{a}$ and $\bar{e}$ are placed very closely against each other, nearly pinching, and held tight; the larynx kept as stiff as possible and placed high.

Vocalises of Clara Kathleen Rogers "Clara Doria"(1844-1931)

Clara Doria was a graduate in composition before becoming a singer. Doria's name before her Italian career was Clara Kathleen Rogers. She attended the Leipzig Conservatory from the age of twelve, sang opera in Italy for ten years, and was steeped in the school of bel canto. She then returned to Boston where she continued to teach, write, as well as compose. I value Clara Doria's work highly and use many of her ideas in my work.

The graph on vowel modification from Clara Doria's work is an eye-opening clarification to the subject. The graph can be found in Doria's book, *The Philosophy of Singing*.[*] The concept of consonant and vowel being produced independently of each other is also invaluable.

* Clara Kathleen Rogers, *The Philosophy of Singing* (Harper and Bros., 1893).

An Exercise in Vowel Modification

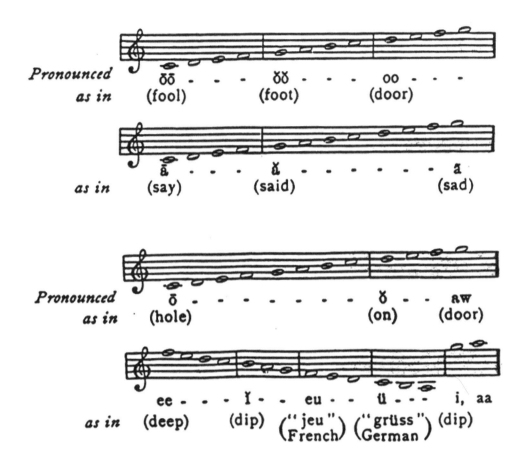

For Enunciating on High Notes

The ability to enunciate on high notes, maintaining clear diction as well as free sound, depends on separating the consonant before the sound is sung.

Example:

First, make the whispered sound <u>sh</u> only, with air in the mouth; then sustain the <u>ah</u>, and finish with <u>oot</u> whispered in the mouth, and then sharply articulate the <u>t</u>.

[Author's note: Observe the following example from Mendelssohn's "Hear Ye Israel." It looks strange, but it is well worth the effort it takes to understand the principle.]

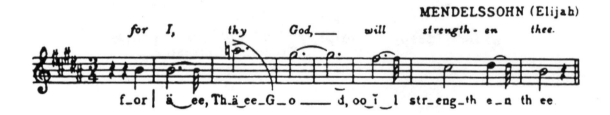

Part 4

Voice Types, Singing Roles, and Learning from the Best

ha vita è breve: la morte viene!....
(più tardi che sia possibile)
Amleto e
Titta Ruffo
1915

Titta Ruffo in the title role of HAMLET by THOMAS.

"Life is short, death comes (as late as possible)."

Introduction to the Voice Types

This section of the book describes each type of voice, and will help the singer find good role models. I advise you to seek out recordings of the singers described herein to become aware of the many colors of the different voice types, and how the most successful of these use the principles described in Part I, The Secrets to Beautiful Singing.

Every singer has a *tessitura*, an area of the voice that is fluid, easy, and of better quality. The range in which this area lies determines the category of the voice. However, there are no hard and fast rules for determining the voice type, and usually other factors come into play.

The first type of female voice is the soprano, of which there are five types: the *lirico leggiero*, the lyric, the *lirico spinto*, the dramatic, and the Wagnerian. I have grouped the lyric and *lirico spinto* sopranos together, and the dramatic and Wagnerian sopranos together, in order to describe certain common elements of these voices and the singers whose repertoires span two or more voice types. Nevertheless, the quality of these voices is very different.

In general, the soprano voice usually is given the romantic parts, but the dramatic and Wagnerian soprano repertoires call for some strong and evil heroines, like MEDÉA of Cherubini, Verdi's Lady Macbeth, ELEKTRA, SALOME, and some Wagnerian roles.

The second type of female voice is the mezzo, or mezzo-soprano. There are two types of mezzos: the lyric mezzo, ideal for Mozart, "pants roles," and especially Rossini and Donizetti roles, and the dramatic mezzo, who sings the heavier Verdi mezzo roles as well as those in Strauss and Wagner.

The third type of female voice is the contralto, the lowest and deepest of the women's voices. Contraltos are rare today, probably due to the few roles available, and perhaps for this reason fewer women singers focus on their deepest and lowest registers and qualities.

The first type of male voice is the tenor, of which there are four types: *leggiero, comprimario, lyric,* and *spinto*. The *leggiero,* or light tenor, has a melting, sweet quality, and is capable of brilliant high notes. The *comprimario* is a "character" tenor with good declamatory style and acting ability, and usually has a smaller voice than a first-string tenor. The *lyric* tenor voice is charismatic and suited to the romantic lead repertoire. The *spinto* is the most powerful tenor, capable of singing the most demanding of the tenor roles.

The baritone voice is generally of two types: The *lyric* baritone is suited to the young lead roles in opera. The color of the voice is light, and this quality lends itself to younger or lighter roles. The Verdi baritone has a heavier and darker quality, suitable to more mature and powerful roles.

The last category of the male voices is the bass, the deepest of the men's voices. Its very dark quality lends itself to serious parts, and sometimes more comic roles.

For each type of singer I describe the voice, give examples of singing roles for that voice type, list who I believe are the best role models, and add any additional advice or comments, if appropriate.

Because there is a great deal of overlapping among the different voice types, and because singers often change voice types as their voices develop over time, and because every voice is unique and some singers defy categorization, I suggest you read the entries for each voice type in your general range.

The Female Voices

The Coloratura Soprano

A Description of the Coloratura Soprano Voice

The highest and lightest of the soprano voices is the coloratura, or *lirico leggiero* as it is called in Italy. This voice is capable of agile runs and decorative trills, as well as an extension as high as F above high C. The coloratura voice is charming, it can be delicate and almost bird-like, and is usually brilliant in its top range.

Some coloraturas develop into more lyric sounds with age, for two reasons: they are no longer suitable for the young ingénue roles in opera, and the color of the voice takes on a more mature sound. However, some coloraturas (examples include Galli-Curci, Tetrazzini, and many of the early Italian singers) retain their youthful color and extensive range.

Roles for the Coloratura Soprano

Because of the lightness and high register of the voice, the music for the young *leggiero* is more suited to the ingénue roles. Rossini, Donizetti, and Bellini have written much music for the *leggiero*. Young girls are usually thought to have this type of voice before they mature.

I started my vocal studies at age sixteen and I was called a coloratura by my teacher, although as my voice matured I became a lyric, and later a *spinto*.

Some roles suited to the coloratura voice are Amina in LA SONNAMBULA, Gilda in RIGOLETTO, Susanna in LE NOZZE DI FIGARO, Despina in COSÌ FAN TUTTE, Zerlina in DON GIOVANNI, Fiorilla in IL TURCO IN ITALIA, and Adina in L'ELISIR D'AMORE, as well roles in many other operas of Donizetti.

A coloratura may develop into more demanding roles and be known as a dramatic coloratura in such parts as the Queen of the Night in Mozart's DIE ZAUBERFLÖTE, or the part of Konstanze in Mozart's DIE ENTFÜHRUNG AUS DEM SERAIL.

Coloratura Soprano Vocal Models

There are many recorded examples of this voice. Of the old singers, there is a wealth to choose from: Adelina Patti, Luisa Tetrazzini (1871-1940), Maria Barrientos (1883-1946), Lily Pons (1904-1976), and Amelita Galli-Curci (1882-1963), as well as Elvira de Hidalgo (1893-1980), the teacher of Maria Callas.

Singers like Maria Callas and Joan Sutherland devoted themselves to a much larger repertoire. They cannot be put into one category because they are unique. For bel canto phrasing, Callas is a model. For pure technical flights in the extreme high voice, Sutherland is extraordinary. I will go into more detail about these singers later.

There are many examples of early singers now on CD. Of the list I mention above, Adelina Patti has the earliest available recording, having made her first recording at age 60, and of course the voice is obviously past its prime. However, she recorded the aria from SONNAMBULA, and it is interesting to realize that she was the closest recorded singer to the time of Bellini.

Nellie Melba was considered a vocal goddess by many, but I frankly do not care for her voice. On the other hand, Luisa Tetrazzini is formidable, even though she is not always musically correct. Her agility is amazing. Amelita Galli-Curci, an Italian soprano, has a very limpid sound. It is birdlike and similar to the voice of Maria Barrientos. Celestina Boninsegna is not well known in this country, but she is an example of a *leggiero* who later developed into a *spinto* soprano. Lina Pagliughi (1907-1980) was a lovely singer whose career took place between 1927 and 1976. She was born in Brooklyn, but was always considered to be an Italian diva. I met her in Milan and watched her teach. She was a very modest lady with a very beautiful color of voice. It was a very good example of the *chiaro-scuro* quality, that is, there was both a light and dark tint in her sound. There are many examples of her singing on the old Cetra recordings of operas.

When I think of great French coloratura sopranos, the name of Lily Pons comes to mind. I began to collect her recordings, old 78s, when I began to study. I loved to *try* to imitate her sound. I heard her LUCIA when I was twelve years old and immediately decided to become an opera singer! I even approached her husband, André Kostelanetz, on a plane trip to Mexico City, plying him with questions about my idol.

The next wonderful soprano is Mady Mesplé. I had the great pleasure of singing my first Pamina to her Queen in DIE ZAUBERFLÖTE, or IL FLAUTO MAGICO, as we performed it at Teatro Bellini in Catania, Sicily. Pictures of us can be found in the Photo Album of the DVD. Mady was also a consummate recitalist. She has many interesting recordings of her French concert repertoire.

**Author (2nd from right) in cast photo with coloratura
soprano Mady Mesplé (left) after performance of
"The Magic Flute" at Teatro Bellini (Italy).**

Mado Robin (1918-1960) was another French soprano with an exceptional range. Her extension was to an A above high C! The voice is not large, but it is very interesting to hear those *sopra-acuti*, as the Italians have named them. Her recordings are rather rare, but they are worth a search. The ruling French coloratura of the day is Natalie Dessay. She is a brilliant singer of many important roles such as LUCIA, Zerbinetta in ARIADNE AUF NAXOS, Ophélie in HAMLET, and the Doll in HOFFMANN. Her performance in this role can be viewed on a DVD made by the Opéra National de Lyon.

There are many other fine European coloraturas, and I suggest you look for their recordings in a library if you are curious. Among them are Olimpia Boronat (1867-1934), Christina Deutekom (Amsterdam 1934), Anneliese Rothenberger (Mannheim, 1924), Erika Köth (Darmstadt, 1927-1989), Rita Streich (Barnaul, 1920-1987), Miliza Korjus (Warsaw, 1907-1980), Edita Gruberova (Bratislava, 1946), and Mariella Devia (Imperia, 1950).

There are a few interesting Americans to hear as well. Roberta Peters was the youngest singer to debut at the Metropolitan as Zerlina in DON GIOVANNI. She was the protégée of the great Russian impresario, Sol Hurok. She was born in 1930 and *still* gives concerts. There is a fine recording of ARIADNE AUF NAXOS with Peters as Zerbinetta. The great dramatic soprano, Leonie Rysanek, sings the title role. Another fine singer, Anna Moffo made her career in Italy when she was very young. She also had her own TV show while I was there. Moffo has many recordings of both opera and arias as well as several video productions. Beverly Sills is a singer who made the most of a talent that is debated by many, but she has enjoyed much acclaim for her expansive repertoire of the Donizetti queens, i.e. ROBERTO DEVEREUX and MARIA STUARDA. She had great success in her La Scala debut in L'ASSEDIO DI CORINTO. I was present that evening and she was brilliant. She has many recordings that are easily available.

Currently, there are two American sopranos that are enjoying big careers. They are Ruth Ann Swenson and Laura Claycomb. Swenson is known for her LUCIA as well as the three parts in HOFFMANN and LA TRAVIATA. She is now starting to develop into a heavier repertoire. Laura Claycomb recently sang a magnificent Gilda in the production of the Houston Grand Opera. Swenson has many recordings, but Claycomb has thus far not yet recorded a solo album and has appeared only in lesser known works or small parts.

Advice to Coloratura Sopranos

The coloratura voice is delicate and special attention must be given to the middle range. The tendency for young coloraturas to prefer singing only in the high range is because it is so much easier for them. But the foundation of every soprano voice is the middle, i.e. middle C to the octave above and on to the E natural or F.

There are several songs of Bellini that are a fine study for the middle voice. They can be found in a collection of his songs published by Ricordi. Two examples are "Vaga luna che inargenti" and "Il fervido desiderio."

Although the basic sound of this voice is clear and slender, this does not mean that there is not a firm connection to the support of the body throughout. The high notes seem detached from the body, but they depend on their center of energy coming from a grounded support from the diaphragm.

The coloratura voice depends on the ease and brilliance in the extreme high notes, and so the study of agility is of greatest importance. The middle voice must be centered and well grounded in order to arrive at the highest notes. I stress a slender approach to the sound, and avoiding the temptation to enlarge the middle voice. *Legato* singing is also very important to building strength in this voice as it is in all types of voices.

The Lyric and Lirico Spinto Sopranos

A Description of the Lyric and Lirico Spinto Soprano Voices

The pure lyric soprano has more depth and color throughout her range than the *leggiero*; the range extends from A below middle C to high D. Her extension is not as high as that of the *leggiero*, and her roles call for more emphasis on emotion and do not generally require as much agility.

Many lyric sopranos develop into the more dramatic type of lyric, the *lirico spinto*. The true *lirico spinto* voice is a borderline Italian dramatic soprano. She has the ability for dramatic accents and the *squillo* brilliance to dominate a large chorus. This does not mean thick or heavy, broad sounds. It means color, flow, and not drive. She, too, must have command of agility.

Roles for the Lyric and Lirico Spinto Soprano

The lyric and *lirico spinto* sopranos are usually best suited to the romantic female leads.

The lyric soprano romantic parts include Mimì in Puccini's LA

BOHÈME, Micaela in Bizet's CARMEN, Suzel in Mascagni's L'AMICO FRITZ, and Juliette in ROMÉO ET JULIETTE of Gounod, to name a few. Verdi's TRAVIATA is sung by many sopranos of different types, but it requires great agility, power, and stamina not always found in a pure *lyric* voice. For example, Mirella Freni was, in her early career, a pure lyric and she was not successful in TRAVIATA, but later developed more toward the *spinto* soprano.

Freni has numerous recordings. Among the most interesting is her famous BOHÈME with Pavarotti. The quality of her voice is most typical of the Italian lyric sound. She was encouraged by von Karajan to sing heavier parts and she had great success as Desdemona in Verdi's OTELLO. She also sang Elisabetta in DON CARLO of Verdi as well as AÏDA. I remember hearing one of her first great successes in the Arena di Verona in Italy. She sang Micaela. She outshone the Carmen, who was a well-known singer from the Metropolitan. Franco Corelli was also in that cast!

I appeared in a season with her in Spain (Bilbao and Oviedo). She sang L'ELISIR D'AMORE with Pavarotti and I sang Elena in Boito's MEFISTOFELE. She was a lovely colleague and very calm and uncomplicated.

There have been many singers who have sung parts in various repertoire categories. It is impossible to set hard and fast rules for each voice. For example, the beloved soprano Licia Albanese had great success in TRAVIATA as well as MADAMA BUTTERFLY of Puccini. She was a brilliant singer with a sure agility, but with an added sense of the dramatic. She is still a charming, dynamic lady who seems to have a great joy in helping young singers. Toscanini said she was his favorite soprano and he used her in his NBC opera broadcast. The TRAVIATA of Toscanini is still available and she also has an aria collection. I have a recording (a 33 rpm) of her MANON LESCAUT of Puccini with Jussi Bjöerling. I doubt if it is still in print.

The parts for the *spinto* voice include Leonora in IL TROVATORE, AÏDA, Amelia in UN BALLO IN MASCHERA, Amelia in SIMONE BOCCANEGRA, TOSCA, and MADAMA BUTTERFLY (for the lyric as well).

There should be no hard and fast rules about the lyric or *lirico spinto*. A singer with agility and extension can sing the Bellini LA SONNAMBULA and I PURITANI, as well as some of the more lyrical roles such as Liù in TURANDOT, Micaela in CARMEN and, depending on the temperament, LA TRAVIATA. She can also sing the title role in ANNA BOLENA of Donizetti as well and other works of Donizetti.

Many parts, like UN BALLO IN MASCHERA, AÏDA, ADRIANA LECOUVREUR, Maddalena in ANDREA CHÉNIER, and LA FANCIULLA DEL WEST, overlap and are performed by a wide range of sopranos. This also depends on the temperament of the singer.

Lyric and Lirico Spinto Soprano Vocal Models

Renata Tebaldi had one of the most beautiful voices I have ever heard. Although by nature a lyric, Tebaldi's was one of the largest sounds on stage. Her Mimì was amazing for its sheer beauty. She sang TOSCA and finally Minnie in LA FANCIULLA DEL WEST, but was less successful in dramatic parts because of her more gentle temperament, and her voice was not at its best on the extremely high notes. *But* the quality! Tebaldi started out as a full lyric who finally sang *spinto*-dramatic roles like LA GIOCONDA.

Virginia Zeani, from Bucharest, is another soprano of note. She began as a lyric soprano, but because of her dramatic talent and excellent technique, she sang more *spinto* roles after a tremendous success in TRAVIATA.

Renata Scotto started out as a *lirico leggiero*, and because of her drive and ambition she essayed many dramatic roles that were very successful, even if not vocally ideal. She had great success at the beginning of her career as Amina in Bellini's SONNAMBULA. As she developed she became a brilliant LUCIA, as well as a heart-rending BUTTERFLY. For me, her video of MANON LESCAUT with Domingo is a marvelous example of her artistry. She pushed herself into roles like Verdi's Lady Macbeth and Abigaille in Verdi's NABUCCO. While she was effective on the stage, she suffered a vocal decline with these roles.

Anna Moffo began her career in Italy in light roles and was very successful in LA TRAVIATA and as Liù in TURANDOT. She was not so successful when she attempted to sing heavier roles. She sang for a time in Germany and in many performances of German light opera. She was an ideal singer of Mozart and also a fine Liù at the Metropolitan Opera.

Mirella Freni began as a lyric and has had an exceptional career. She started with Mimì and Micaela, and proceeded to sing Desdemona in OTELLO, BUTTERFLY, AÏDA, ADRIANA LECOUVREUR, and at present Tatiana in EUGENE ONEGIN and FEDORA.

In the American wing of singers there are many fine lyric sopranos. One of the earliest was Geraldine Farrar (1882-1967). She was a great beauty and often sang with Caruso. Grace Moore (1901-1947) was another glamorous soprano who was more noted for her movies than for an exceptional voice. Her protégée was Dorothy Kirsten (1917-1992), who shared many of the same roles with Licia Albanese. There are recordings of all these singers.

Another fine lyric soprano, who sang only briefly in the US, is Marcella Pobbé (1927 - 2003). I heard her in person only once. She was a beautiful woman and her voice was limpid but rather cool. She sang with Mario Del Monaco and Tito Gobbi in a performance in the courtyard of the Palazzo Del Doge in Venice. It was an unforgettable performance and she seemed to be the ideal Desdemona to the clarion voice of Del Monaco as Verdi's OTELLO. She has two marvelous recitals of arias on a Cetra CD. I am sad to record her passing away in 2003.

Another of the bel canto style lyric sopranos is Montserrat Caballé. Her melting *piano* singing was her forte and she essayed many roles of Donizetti at the start of her career. She, too, sang many of the heavier roles later in her career. But her main interest was the sheer beauty of the sound, and this made her a rather static singer on stage. I appeared in a season in Spain with her when she sang in IL TROVATORE. She was a fine example of the bel canto school, and years later she was magnificent in an all-Wagner concert in New York City.

Magda Olivero has had such a long career that she sang Liù in the first complete recording of TURANDOT. In her 50s, she finally debuted at the Metropolitan. Olivero was a great lady of the stage. I had the privilege of knowing her and being her understudy in Poulenc's LA VOIX HUMAINE on one occasion. She was kind, giving, and one of the most intense singers I have ever heard onstage. Ciléa adored her and said she was his ideal ADRIANA LECOUVREUR. On recordings her voice has a tremulous quality that is not so apparent in the flesh. In her 80s, after retirement, she recorded an abridged version of ADRIANA made at La Scala in a large *sala*. Her cast was made up of young singers and there were moments of greatness evident in the performance. It is worth hearing! I was present in Bergamo when she returned after some years in silence (this was before her Met debut). She sang ADRIANA and I taped it on a tiny cassette recorder. It was a lesson in complete dedication and focus.

Another interesting soprano who achieved much success in Italy was the Turkish-born Leyla Gencer. She had a very extensive repertoire that included Gilda in Verdi's RIGOLETTO, Mozart roles, as well as the *spinto* roles of Verdi and Donizetti. She also sang Santuzza in CAVALLERIA RUSTICANA, as well as the title roles in SUOR ANGELICA and NORMA.

Other more lyric voices are Nuccia Focile and Ileana Cotrubas. Of the old singers, I recommend listening to Mafalda Favero (1905-1981), a brilliant singer-actress. Listening to recordings of *all* these singers is an invaluable way to develop a keen ear for beautiful sound. The late Bidu Sayao was a beautiful lyric with great stage charm in that repertoire.

Among the *spinto* sopranos, Elizabeth Rethberg was a perfect example. Claudia Muzio (1889-1936) came from a theater family and she grew up in that environment. She began in a lighter role, Massenet's MANON, but sang all the more *spinto* roles from TRAVIATA through TOSCA and NORMA. She was electric on the stage and had great success both in America and Europe. My teacher, Luisa Pallazzini, was her successor and sang many performances in companies with her. Muzio has numerous recordings, the best of which are the Marston Collections. Her voice was of a rare quality that expressed all the *chiaroscuro* color associated with the Italian sound. She was often compared to the great Italian actress, Eleonora Duse, and the first to be called "La Divina."

Other voices of this type in the last 25 years are Leontyne Price and Montserrat Caballé (mentioned earlier). The Croatian soprano, Zinka Milanov, was one of the most important *spintos* in the 40s and 50s. She, like Montserrat, possessed one of the most haunting *pianissimos* ever heard.

Lotte Lehmann (1885-1976) is another singer I recommend as a voice model, although she had a very large repertoire and is one of those singers who defies classification. I studied and performed the part of the Marschallin under her direction in Santa Barbara at the Music Academy of the West. Mme. Lehmann sang the entire Italian repertoire in Germany before coming to America. She later sang Wagner and, of course, Strauss. She sang performances of TURANDOT in Germany, but told me it was not the ideal part vocally or temperamentally.

As a final word, there is another very charismatic singer whom I used to see on the front row of the Met when she was very elderly. She was always swathed in furs and diamonds and wore a large picture hat. She was Maria Jeritza (1887-1982), another favorite of Puccini. She sang a large repertoire, from the lighter roles to the more lyric Wagner roles. She was well known for her TURANDOT in Vienna. My impression from Lotte Lehmann, whenever Jeritza's name came up, was that they were unprofessed rivals. They were both favorites of Puccini and Strauss and often created Strauss roles. Jeritza created the role of TOSCA for Puccini. The story goes that at the dress rehearsal of TOSCA, Jeritza fell in the second act during the scene in which Scarpia was attacking her.

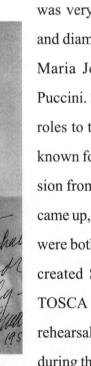

Lotte Lehmann

As she fell, her long blonde hair came loose and as she lay there, she began to sing "Vissi D'arte." Puccini requested that she repeat this at the Premiere. She had phenomenal success in the role.

Lotte Lehmann told me that she felt Tosca was too theatrical a piece for her, although she did follow Jeritza in that part. I have a taped interview of the two of them together long after they no longer performed. They were playful and charming on the surface, but there was no doubt that they were not close.

A whole chapter could be devoted to another remarkable *spinto*, the dynamic and brilliant Rosa Ponselle (1897-1981). I was brought up on 78-rpm recordings of hers. My first teacher of singing insisted that I make a study of them. At any hour of the day and night the sound of her ERNANI recording or CASTA DIVA could be heard coming from my room. Her sense of line, color, and her technical ability caused Caruso to call her, in their Neapolitan dialect, "*Caruso in gonnella*"... Caruso in a skirt. He was instrumental in having her debut with him at the Metropolitan Opera in her early twenties. She even fainted at her audition and was still hired!

I never dreamed at sixteen that when I was in my early twenties I would travel to Stevenson, Maryland, to sing for Rosa Ponselle...much less to have lessons! She had retired years before, but maintained her voice and was able to demonstrate while teaching. To expe-

Rosa Ponselle in the library of her Stevenson, MD home.

Rosa Ponselle as Carmen.

rience the sound of her voice at close range was a great lesson in itself. It was powerful, never thick, and it was produced with a completely even scale. I had grown up with her recording of Casta Diva, but to hear it at a range of several feet was like a dream. (I have included some of the exercises in the vocalise section.) Like Muzio, Ponselle's voice had the haunting color of *chiaro-scuro*. She decided to record songs for RCA on her own terms and in her home, Villa Pace. These recordings have been released on CD and I think they should be heard by all young singers. They are a lesson in *legato*. The video entitled "The Art of Singing" is also a "must." Her CARMEN arias are thrilling, and there are also many other fine singers of the past to be heard in the video.

I should also like to include the young soprano, Angela Gheorghiu. She has an important voice and was featured in the film production of LA TRAVIATA conducted by the late Georg Solti. She is very communicative in her phrasing and at times bears a strong resemblance to Maria Callas' manner of phrasing. There is also a new video of L'ELISIR D'AMORE in which she sings opposite her husband, Roberto Alagna. She recently has delved into a heavier repertoire such as TROVATORE and a splendid film version of Puccini's TOSCA.

Kiri Te Kanawa is a formidable singer of Richard Strauss. Her ARABELLA and CAPRICCIO are very moving. She has a seamless voice for the high-lying Strauss phrases. Marjorie Lawrence was also a fine singer of Strauss. In the *lirico* or *lirico-spinto* category, Miriam Gauci is a younger singer to hear. She is from Malta. For me, she is a vocal "find." She records for the Naxos label. She has a solo album and has also recorded MADAMA BUTTERFLY, MANON LESCAUT, and SIMONE BOCCANEGRA, among other works.

Currently, there is a singer who is said to have the most beautiful soprano voice today. She is Renée Fleming. She began her career with Mozart in the role of the Countess in the MARRIAGE OF FIGARO and has sung many roles in both the lyric and *spinto* repertoires. In the last few years she has developed a repertoire that seems to span all types of operatic music from the modern operas such as A STREET-CAR NAMED DESIRE by André Previn to Strauss' ARABELLA, the Marschallin in DER ROSENKAVALIER, also by Richard Strauss, and Tatiana in EUGENE ONEGIN. She recently had a great success in three very different roles: THAÏS by Massenet, the bel canto tour de force of Bellini, IL PIRATA, and most recently in her first TRAVIATA. I was present at each of those performances and I concur that she is all they say. She really is a master of her voice and she uses it with complete dedication for communicating the meaning of the text as well as creating exceptional sounds. I believe she has one of the most perfect vocal techniques and her many recordings testify to this. I highly recommend them. It is impossible to categorize her voice and this is usually true for most exceptional singers.

Advice for Lyric and Lirico Spinto Sopranos

The lyric soprano must be wise in not pushing her voice into the more *spinto* repertoire if she does not have a sizeable voice and the stamina required by more dramatic roles. Freni, for example, did not begin with a *spinto* repertoire but allowed her voice to mature into it. Two other factors enter here: they are the size of the orchestra and the size of the theater. The study and style for both types of sopranos are the same.

Leontyne Price had an ideal *spinto* sound at the outset of her career, yet she had the extension of a more lyric soprano. For me, her singing of the VERDI REQUIEM with von Karajan in Salzburg was the perfect performance. She was a great AÏDA, Leonora in

TROVATORE, and a superb Mozart singer. She was equally at home in concerts. In fact, I was present at her last Carnegie recital (just released on CD) and she was spectacular.

The true *lirico spinto* voice is usually one that sings the Verdi repertoire that Price sang. She may also sing MADAMA BUTTERFLY, TOSCA (Puccini), IL TABARRO, and SUOR ANGELICA (both Puccini). Another versatile *spinto* was Raina Kabaivanska. She has had a long career and can be seen in many video productions, including TOSCA with Pavarotti.

Recordings

It is difficult to give a list of recordings for many of the singers I have mentioned because the earlier ones have much material that is no longer in the catalogues, but I think that a search would be invaluable. Of the ones that are readily available, I recommend Rosa Ponselle, Caballé, Leontyne Price, Mirella Freni, Ileana Cotrubas, and Angela Gheorghiu. I have listed others in the section for dramatic sopranos.

Before I leave this section of sopranos, I want to mention two other very fine sopranos who are *spintos*. They are Barbara Frittoli and Adrianne Pieczonka. Frittoli is a lovely Italian soprano who can be heard in a recording of TURANDOT as Liù, as well as in a recording of IL TROVATORE, and in a fine concert of Mozart arias. Pieczonka is a Canadian with a beautiful recording in an album of Strauss Orchestral Songs on the Nightingale label and a fine Donna Anna in DON GIOVANNI on the Naxos label. She also sings a delightful Rosalinda in the FLEDERMAUS recording for Nightingale. Both of these singers have splendid vocal techniques and they are very communicative in their singing.

The Dramatic and Wagnerian Sopranos

A Description of the Dramatic and Wagnerian Soprano Voices

The major difference between the dramatic and Wagnerian sopranos and the sopranos previously mentioned is not only the roles they sing, but the color of their voices. The dramatic soprano is darker and more similar in sound to the *mezzo*—it is *brunito*, or penetrating; it cuts through the orchestra like nothing. The Wagnerian soprano is likewise darker and it is the most powerful voice of all the sopranos.

In comparison, the *spinto* is usually lighter in color, has greater agility, and has a wider range of dynamics in *piano* and *mezza-voce*.

Roles for Dramatic and Wagnerian Sopranos

It is almost impossible to draw a hard line between a *spinto* and a dramatic soprano. They share some roles depending not only on the color of the voice, but the temperament. The true dramatic soprano is capable of singing the *spinto* repertoire as well, but this voice can also sing Wagner and Strauss. She is often cast in roles of strong or evil heroines, like MEDÉA of Cherubini, ELEKTRA, and SALOME. Of the Italian repertoire, the heaviest parts of Verdi, such as Abigaille in NABUCCO and Lady Macbeth, are more suited to the dramatic soprano. The dramatic soprano who sings the Italian repertoire sometimes does roles in Wagner as well.

The Wagnerian soprano, of course, sings all the Wagner Brünhildes.

Dramatic and Wagnerian Soprano Vocal Models

The true dramatic voices are all too rare. Kirsten Flagstad (1895-1962) was one of these. She also sang light music as a beginner and even did some operetta in Norway. I read an article in which she said that she discovered the key to her real voice and its power when she learned about the "valve" closure in the throat. (Does this sound familiar?) Flagstad was known for her Brünhildes in the DER RING DES NIBELUNGEN tetralogy, and for her Kundry in PARSIFAL. When she was first heard in an audition for the Met, they were under the impression that she did not have a large voice. With an orchestra, it was quite another matter.

Helen Traubel (1898-1972) was an American soprano who had fine success in the same operas. Eileen Farrell (1920-2002) was an American who had a truly beautiful voice capable of the *spinto* Verdi roles as well as Wagner. She was a singer of songs for years before developing into a fine exponent of the Italian repertoire as well as French and German roles. She has a fine solo CD, as well as a recital of duets with Richard Tucker.

Other sopranos who have sung both *spinto* and dramatic roles are the fabled Lilli Lehmann (1848-1929), who sang Mozart as well as all the heaviest Wagner. The late Leonie Rysanek was a consummate singer who accepted the part of Lady Macbeth when Callas left the Metropolitan. She was magnificent and can be heard on a recording of that time with Leonard Warren. Her greatest successes were in Strauss: the Empress in DIE FRAU OHNE SCHATTEN, and ARIADNE AUF NAXOS. I studied with a very famous dramatic soprano, Germaine Lubin (1890-1979). She was also the teacher of the French soprano, Régine Crespin, who was also a brilliant singer of Wagner, but started in the Italian repertoire. She, too, has many recordings. Lubin sang the entire dramatic repertoire from Mozart to Wagner.

Emmy Destinn (1878-1930) is another of the dramatic voices from the time of Caruso. She does not record well because of the recordings made at that time, but her voice was said to rival that of Caruso. In fact, she sang the premiere of LA FANCIULLA DEL WEST (Minnie) opposite Caruso at the Metropolitan Opera.

The English woman, Eva Turner (1892-1990), was also an outstanding singer of this repertoire. Her recording of "In Questa Reggia" from TURANDOT is one that I had on an old 78 recording. Her high C was so powerful that the needle would nearly jump off its track! It can be found on CD. The earlier Wagnerian sopranos who recorded in Germany were Frieda Leider, Rosa Pauly (also a fine singer of Strauss), Meta Seinemeyer, Johanna

Germaine Lubin

Gadski, Göte Ljungberg, Margaret Teschemacher, and Maria Müller.*

Most of the ladies mentioned above also sang operas of Richard Strauss. Lotte Lehmann (described in the *spinto* section, although she also sang dramatic and Wagnerian roles) has a recording of Act I of DIE WALKÜRE, as well as a recital of various arias from Wagner.

Callas and Sutherland—two distinctly different yet unique singers

No work about singers could be complete without noting the effect that Maria Callas (1923-1977) had on the world of opera. She was unique. It was not the most beautiful voice, but it was riveting due to her musical integrity and command of the stage. I heard her Chicago lyric debut in NORMA. She was already thin by then and her voice was still in perfect order. Her singing of the "Casta Diva," the duets with Simionato, and the final phrases, "In mia man alfin tu sei," will always be with me. Several days later she sang LA TRAVIATA there in Chi-

---

* These voices can be heard on HMV's "Record of Singing," Vol. 3. From a historical standpoint, it would be helpful to hear the entire series. Unfortunately, the last volume is the only one to be found on CD so far.

cago. Her voice sounded completely different... a shadow of the Norma voice. I wondered if she were ill, and in fact she was quoted later as intending to sound consumptive.

I was present at Callas' Master Classes at Juilliard. As an auditor in the front row, I observed her at close range. MASTER CLASS, the play of Terence McNally, portrayed her as bitter and critical. I am sure that there were liberties he took for the sake of the play, but we did not see that side of her there. She demanded discipline of the singers, as she surely demanded it from herself, but she was encouraging and patient while coaxing and inspiring the singers to grow in their craft.

Joan Sutherland sang much of Callas' repertoire. She can be heard with Callas as Clotilde, her confidant, in the early recording of NORMA from Covent Garden. Sutherland specialized in the very early florid bel canto repertoire. From a technical standpoint she was phenomenal, producing a large and seemingly effortless sound. She was totally unknown at her Paris debut in LUCIA DI LAMMERMOOR, and within the week she was on her way to becoming a great star. I was living in Paris at the time and after her debut I went to the box office to buy seats for all the other performances. Her gift was not the communication of the dramatic meaning of the text, and this was accepted because of the beauty and amazing ease with which she could sing the most difficult music.

Birgit Nilsson is the last of the great dramatic sopranos to date. She sang a vast number of roles before dedicating herself to Wagner. She sang Elettra from IDOMENEO, as well as the operas of Strauss, along with SALOME, Minnie in LA FANCIULLA, TOSCA, and her "vacation role" as she called it, TURANDOT! Although she is retired and only does Master Classes, I've heard that she still can sing the Queen of the Night from DIE ZAUBERFLÖTE, the high F's and all.

Deborah Voigt seems the ideal soprano to follow the ladies mentioned above. She has recorded an excellent ARIADNE.

Astrid Varnay is also a very important dramatic soprano whose career encompasses both the Italian repertoire as well as the Wagnerian and Strauss roles. She was also successful in CARMEN, which she sang often with Franco Corelli. Her recordings of excerpts from Wagner's RING are marvelous. Her partner is the noted Wagnerian tenor, Wolfgang Windgassen. Her repertoire included such varied roles as ELEKTRA, Isolde, Lady Macbeth, and AÏDA. She was a reigning soprano in the 1950s.

Another interesting and brilliant soprano is Julia Varady. She has sung all the Italian repertoire of Puccini as well as the *jügenlich dramatisch* roles of Wagner. She recorded a whole evening of Wagner with Peter Seiffert, an excellent tenor, conducted by her husband Dietrich Fischer-Dieskau, the renowned lieder baritone. The most surprising of her work is a recording of Puccini's EDGAR made in 2002. She was born in 1941, but she is splendid and sounds like a young woman.

Karita Mattila is a young dramatic soprano from Scandinavia. She is able to encompass both *spinto* and dramatic roles by virtue of her exceptional instrument and her dramatic temperament onstage. She has numerous recordings.

Additional Points for Dramatic and Wagnerian Sopranos

The temptation for young singers is to be persuaded by managers and record companies to take on dramatic repertoire before they have the maturity of voice to encompass these roles. But the result of over-singing can produce vocal fatigue and, ultimately, a sound that wobbles. I hope that the wonderful young soprano, Renée Fleming, will not be tempted to sing such a heavy repertoire. Her voice is of such a beautiful quality that she would be unwise to sacrifice it for sheer volume.

Of the Italian repertoire, the heaviest parts of Verdi, such as Abigaille in NABUCCO and Lady Macbeth, are more suited to the dramatic soprano, and many great singers, like Callas and Scotto, have sung these parts more or less successfully, but have paid a high vocal price.

The Mezzo-Sopranos—Lyric and Dramatic

A Description of the Mezzo-Soprano Voice

There are basically two types of mezzo-soprano voices. The lyric mezzo has a more slender sound and is happiest in the range of A below middle C, and up to a high C in certain roles. This voice is mellow, and capable of fine agility and much charm. Many lyric mezzos develop into the heavier, dramatic roles with time. The dramatic mezzo is a more powerful voice, and one that has a superior range from a low G below middle C, and up to B flat above the staff.

Roles for the Mezzo-Soprano

The lyric mezzo sings Mozart, Cherubino in FIGARO, Handel, I CAPULETI E I MONTECCHI of Bellini (Romeo), and numerous "pants roles."

The dramatic mezzo can encompass the big roles of Verdi: Azucena in IL TROVATORE, Amneris in AÏDA, and Ulrica in UN BALLO IN MASCHERA, as well as Eboli in DON CARLO, Laura in LA GIOCONDA, CARMEN, Santuzza in CAVALLERIA RUSTICANA (sung by both sopranos and mezzo-sopranos), and Lady Macbeth. Lady Macbeth was sung by three great mezzo-sopranos: Elena Nikolaidi, Irene Dalis, and Christa Ludwig.

Mezzo-Soprano Vocal Models

A prime example of the more lyric mezzo is the voice of Fiorenza Cossotto, whom I first heard sing Cimarosa at La Scala, and Preziozilla in LA FORZA DEL DESTINO at the Arena in Verona. She later developed into a true Verdi dramatic mezzo.

One of my favorite mezzos of the lighter type is Teresa Berganza. She is also a consummate singer of songs, as well.

Two of the most appealing lyric mezzos of today are Frederica Von Stade and, of course, Cecilia Bartoli. Von Stade really grew up at the Metropolitan and has continued to develop as an exceptional artist, both in opera and concert literature. Her many recordings attest to her exceptional artistry. Bartoli, on the other hand, arrived like a meteor with very strong publicity that preceded her American debut. She has been criticized for the small size of her voice, and her technique in agility is both astounding and very manipulated, but she is an extraordinary communicator. I have heard her both in opera and concert and am always amazed at the way she phrases and her ability to sing the meaning of the text. Her CD of Old Italian songs is a very important example of her artistry. She, of course, can be seen on numerous videos of both opera and concert.

A good mezzo of the heavier, dramatic type is Giulietta Simionato. The amazing thing is that she began singing bit parts at La Scala and rose to the top in her field. I shall always remember hearing her Azucena in IL TROVATORE in Salzburg with Leontyne Price, Corelli, and Ettore Bastianini. This was opera at its grandest.*

Olga Borodina is the current "star" mezzo in this repertoire. She has wonderful CDs and has phenomenal agility, even for Rossini, al-

---

* The live recording exists on CD now and it is worth hearing. Von Karajan conducts.

though she also performs the dramatic repertoire.

Denyce Graves has also developed into a formidable mezzo. She has continued to make great strides in her career and has a very fine voice as well as a stunning stage presence. Her Delilah in SAMSON is brilliant, and that together with her CARMEN are her signature roles.

Dolora Zajick is a remarkable mezzo-soprano who is able to sing all the great dramatic roles in opera. Her voice is reminiscent of the great mezzos who recorded in Italy in the 1940s. I first heard her as Amneris in the opening of the new Wortham Center by the Houston Grand Opera. Her final scene was thrilling! Her voice has a dark color, but maintains the brilliance necessary to penetrate even the largest orchestra with clarity. I recommend her CD of arias, which was conducted by my dear friend and colleague, Charles Rosekrans.

Of course, no list of mezzos would be complete without Marilyn Horne. She was to the bel canto mezzo repertoire what Joan Sutherland represented to the sopranos. Not only did she excel in that repertoire, but she was a marvelous concert artist. Her lieder recitals were always sold out. She now dedicates herself to helping young singers and her direction at the Music Academy of the West in Santa Barbara is formidable.

Risë Stevens was an ideal Octavian in DER ROSENKAVALIER, and had a repertoire ranging from CARMEN to DELILAH. She can be heard on CD as well as seen in the newly released video, "The Art of Singing." She made several movies with such stars as Bing Crosby and Nelson Eddy.

Frances Bible was my first Octavian when I sang the Marschallin. She was a fine singer-actress with a technique that enabled her to sing LA CENERENTOLA as well as the pants roles, Amneris in AÏDA, and the part of Augusta in THE BALLAD OF BABY DOE (she was the first to sing the role at the premiere).

Blanche Thebom was certainly one of the most exciting and beautiful mezzos I ever heard onstage. She was as at home in the dramatic part of Amneris as she was a charming Dorabella in Mozart's COSÌ FAN TUTTE. I'll never forget her final scene as Amneris in AÏDA as she ran up a steep stairway while singing the perilous phrase ending in a high B flat.

There are other mezzos to hear in the repertoire calling for agility. They are Jennifer Larmore and Vesselina Kasarova, as well as Susan Graham. Another brilliant singer is Anne Sophie von Otter. She is a marvelous Octavian in DER ROSENKAVALIER as well as a consummate lieder singer, as is her predecessor, Christa Ludwig.

Elena Nikolaidi

Additional Comments for the Mezzo-Soprano

The tendency for the young ambitious mezzo is to over-darken the sound and thicken it in the middle range. This gives the sound artificially added color. It certainly shortens their vocal life. The more dramatic mezzo has a naturally darker sound and the study should be devoted to an even scale in weight and color throughout. Of course, this is the "ideal" for all voices.

Frances Bible

The Contralto

A Description of the Contralto Voice

The contralto is the lowest and deepest of the female voices. The contralto range can extend to an A above the staff and down to a low E or F below middle C, and is distinguished by a dark sound.

There are generally two types of contralto: First, there is the voice that sings church music, cantatas, and early operas such as those of Monteverdi. Secondly, there are the contralto voices that overlap the repertoire of the dramatic mezzo.

Voices of this type seem to be quite rare today. In fact it is hard to imagine how few of these voices now exist—voices like Ernestine Schumann-Heink. Perhaps this is because historically women singers have tended to focus less on their deepest and lowest registers and qualities; or perhaps composers have set the trend by creating few female roles with this quality.

Roles for the Contralto

Roles for the contralto include Azucena in IL TROVATORE, Mother in THE CONSUL, Orsini in LUCREZIA BORGIA, Ulrica in UN BALLO IN MASCHERA, and the pants role, Orfeo, from ORFEO ED EURIDICE. Handel also wrote many works for the contralto voice.

Mezzo-sopranos and contraltos often sing each other's roles. This is due to the lack of this heavier type of voice.

Contralto Vocal Models

In the days of Caruso, the most noted contralto was Ernestine Schumann-Heink (1861-1936). Recordings do not give a good idea of her voice. It sounds muted and wooly, but I am sure that it was a remarkable voice. Louise Homer was a peer of hers and she, too, seems to suffer from recordings.

The Scandinavian Sigrid Onegin has some very interesting recordings showing beautiful color and agility as she sings the Brindisi from LUCREZIA BORGIA. The voice seems very slender and her technique is very Italianate in its sound.

Marian Anderson was a very special singer and her main career was in concerts, although she did sing Ulrica in UN BALLO IN MASCHERA late in her career. The unique sound lent itself much more to intimate music. She was a soulful artist and opened many doors for other great black artists like Leontyne Price, Shirley Verrett, Grace Bumbry, Jessye Norman, Denyce Graves, and Barbara Hendricks.

Fedora Barbieri is the only true contralto I have ever heard in person. She had a dark but brilliant sound and was a superb actress as well. She can be heard on several re-releases on CD. They are worth the search. She, too, passed on recently.

Gianna Pederzini and Maria Gay are other singers who did both the mezzo and contralto repertoire. They, too, are very impressive.

The English are noted for the contralto voices, but I find the sound to be deep and very straight, which sounds more at home in the repertoire of oratorio. Kathleen Ferrier and Janet Baker are two of the best.

Maureen Forrester is a contralto of note and has a large number of recordings of lieder and some orchestral works. She has sung very little opera.

Currently, the closest sound to the contralto is that of Stephanie Blythe. She also has great agility and stage presence. She reminds me of Marilyn Horne, but her voice seems much more naturally produced.

The Male Voices

The Leggiero Tenor

A Description of the Leggiero Tenor Voice

The light tenor, or *leggiero*, has a melting sweet quality, but it is also capable of brilliant high notes. Although it is high, this voice does not resemble the *castrato*, which is closer to a mezzo. The strong point of the *leggiero* voice is the dynamic of the *pianissimo*. This type of tenor has an extensive range, is greatly agile, and can sing brilliant scales.

Roles for the Leggiero Tenor

The *leggiero* tenor is ideal for the bel canto repertoire of Rossini, Donizetti, Bellini, Handel, and Mozart. These include such roles as the Count of Almaviva in IL BARBIERE DI SIVIGLIA, Elvino in LA SONNAMBULA, and Tonio in LA FILLE DU RÉGIMENT.

Leggiero Tenor Vocal Models

Examples of the *leggiero* voice are Tito Schipa, Raul Giménez, and Luigi Alva, with whom I often sang. Alfredo Kraus was also this type of tenor, but proceeded to sing more lyric repertoire throughout his very long career.

Leggiero tenor Luigi Alva with the author, backstage after COSÌ FAN TUTTE at Teatro Verdi (Italy)

Rossini and Mozart operas are ideal for the first three voices, but Kraus was able to encompass the heavier parts like FAUST and WERTHER.

Juan Diego Flórez is the new singer doing this repertoire. He has exceptional agility and is a true model of the bel canto school. He has numerous recordings.

Additional Comments for Leggiero Tenors

The tenor voice, like the soprano, has several categories. Some tenors have the ability to sing a wide variety of repertoire. This depends largely on the singer's artistry, skill, and sense of drama. Nevertheless, the singer must not be tempted to force the sound for mere volume at the expense of ruining the beauty of the sound.

The Comprimario Tenor

A Description of the Comprimario Tenor Voice

The character tenor, or *comprimario*, as he is called in Italian, requires a good declamatory style and a keen sense of the stage, or acting ability. The *comprimario* is very revered in Italy. This second tenor has a smaller voice and is lacking in the charismatic beauty of the first-string tenor. He is usually smaller in stature and has a voice which lends itself to character roles.

Roles for the Comprimario Tenor

The *comprimario* is usually given either comic parts or the part of the conniving villain.

Second-lead tenor parts, such as confidants, servants, comic roles, and villainous roles often fall into this category. Roles like Goro in

MADAMA BUTTERFLY, Spoleto in TOSCA, Monostatos in DIE ZAUBERFLÖTE, or L'Incredibile in ANDREA CHÉNIER are important character tenor roles requiring good acting ability and a practiced declamatory style.

Comprimario Tenor Vocal Models

I have sung with a couple of these specialists: Florindo Andreolli and Mario Guggia. Some well-known *comprimarios* are Nico Castel, Piero de Palma, Joseph Frank, Joseph Anthony, and Anthony Laciura.

Comprimario tenor Joseph Perniciaro as Goro in **MADAMA BUTTERFLY**

Nico Castel is a good friend of mine. He is a wonderful singer, as well as a brilliant coach for young aspiring singers in many companies including the Metropolitan Opera. His books of the translations of many operas are invaluable guides for the student.

The Lyric Tenor

A Description of the Lyric Tenor Voice

The lyric tenor is the voice of the romantic lead. He has an extensive range which allows him to exhibit special effects in dynamics as well as compelling climactic high notes.

Roles for the Lyric Tenor

The lyric tenor voice is adapted to the romantic lead repertoire. This tenor sings Massenet's MANON, the Duke in RIGOLETTO, Alfredo in LA TRAVIATA, Edgardo in LUCIA DI LAMMERMOOR, FAUST, and Pinkerton in MADAMA BUTTERFLY.

As he develops, the lyric tenor may proceed on to the heavier lyric parts such as Riccardo in UN BALLO IN MASCHERA and Don José in CARMEN. What makes these roles heavy lyric tenor roles as opposed to *spinto* tenor roles? The *spinto* tenor roles demand declamatory power and great strength in the climaxes and high notes, because they are competing with the orchestra; whereas this is detrimental to the lyric tenor voice.

Lyric Tenor Vocal Models

Among the old singers there is of course Enrico Caruso (1873-1921). But Caruso is unique—he was able to encompass roles from the lyric to the dramatic. I think the best way to understand his voice is to listen to the smooth movement between the vowels and the overall consistency of the color between high and low sounds.

Aureliano Pertile (1885-1952) was known as Toscanini's favorite interpreter while the conductor reigned at La Scala. His voice is not immediately appealing to us today—it seems less beautiful; but listen for a few bars and you will hear a great artist.

Beniamino Gigli (1890-1957) was able to sing the lyric as well as the dramatic repertoire because he did it with his voice in a natural way without forcing for the effects of the *spinto* tenor. He has been criticized for too much sobbing in his interpretations, but the sheer beauty of the sound is wonderful. One of my teachers in Italy conducted the last two performances Gigli sang in Milano. He was in his 60s and sang both CAVALLERIA RUSTICANA and I PAGLIACCI in a double bill. This was at an outdoor performance at the Castello Sforzesco. The conductor, Alfredo Strano, said it was magnificent. Gigli started as a lyric and proceeded to the *spinto* roles, such as Radames in AÏDA, ANDREA CHÉNIER, and IL TROVATORE.

Ferruccio Tagliavini (1913-1995) was another tenor in the style of Gigli. He had the ability to sing marvelous *piano* sounds and yet sing a heavier repertoire as well. His understanding of bel canto was exemplary.

Beniamino Gigli

Fritz Wunderlich (1930-1966) was another wonderful lyric tenor; unfortunately his career was cut short by his early death. His Mozart was especially fine.

More recently, the Swedish tenor Nicolai Gedda is a consummate stylist and has had great success in the lyric repertoire. For me, his Elvino in LA SONNAMBULA with Sutherland at La Scala was a triumph, as was his FAUST there. He is also a wonderful concert artist and is equally at home in all styles and languages.

Carlo Bergonzi has often been called the ideal Verdi tenor, and his long career attests to his vocal technique. If we speak of the *passaggio*, he has mastered this principle perfectly. He was able to encompass a large repertoire ranging from the lighter roles like L'ELISIR D'AMORE to the dramatic Verdi roles and the *verismo* role of Canio in I PAGLIACCI. After becoming familiar with the vowel modification principle you can observe the skill with which Bergonzi uses it.

There are some new voices that I have never heard in the theater, but who have impressive credits. Among them is Ben Heppner, who is very successful in his ANDREA CHÉNIER arias and also in LA FORZA DEL DESTINO. His LOHENGRIN CD is also very fine.

Ramón Vargas is a very fine young tenor from Mexico. He has sung the lighter roles, but now is venturing into a heavier repertoire.

He has sung both HOFFMANN and WERTHER. He has a fine technique and is equally at home in songs. His recording of "Arie Antiche" is a model of bel canto singing.

Additional Comments on the Lyric Tenor Voice

It is well worth mentioning Giuseppe Di Stefano. He is a Sicilian who had one of the most beautiful natural voices I've ever heard. He began as a lyric tenor, but his dramatic temperament drove him to a repertoire that was much too heavy for his basic lyric sound. He began with Massenet's MANON and L'ELISIR D'AMORE, and then he forced himself into parts like IL TROVATORE, CAVALLERIA RUSTICANA, and ANDREA CHÉNIER. He pushed for dramatic effects, and in so doing he spread the sound in the middle, causing him to lose his high notes, which then sounded strident and too open. It is very important to listen to his early recordings of the arias from MIGNON (Thomas) and MANON (Massenet), as well as a live recording of "Salut Demeure" from FAUST.

Among newer tenors, Roberto Alagna has certainly made a place for himself in the lyric repertoire. He, like many others, is being pushed by the record companies to make a big name, as was José Carreras. Like Di Stefano, Carreras was lured into a heavy repertoire that cost him much of his vocal beauty, even before his unfortunate illness.

I could name many young tenors who were on the stage when I sang in Italy and most of them lasted only a short time because they attempted a repertoire that was not for their voices. No doubt this was either from a lack of schooling or pressure to "arrive," no matter what the cost. Franco Bonisolli was one of the few that was able to proceed even to the very heavy roles after beginning as Alfredo in LA TRAVIATA. He, too, passed away in 2003.

The Spinto Tenor

A Description of the Spinto Tenor Voice

The *spinto*, also called a dramatic tenor, is a powerful voice capable of sustaining the largest and most demanding of the tenor roles. This voice must have great strength in the middle voice, as well as top notes that can be heard easily over a large orchestra.

The Italianate *spinto* must be able to sing in a higher range with many B flats and some high Cs. His voice sounds more slender and dominates high-ranging ensembles in the operas.

Roles for the Spinto Tenor

The heaviest Verdi parts are reserved for the real *spinto* tenor. These are Radames in AÏDA, ERNANI, OTELLO, and Alvaro in LA FORZA DEL DESTINO. Roles of other composers include Giordano's ANDREA CHÉNIER, Enzo in Ponchielli's LA GIOCONDA and, of course, Calaf in Puccini's TURANDOT.

The *spinto* repertoire also includes the *heldentenor* (heroic tenor) roles of Wagner. The Wagnerian tenor *tessitura* is nearer that of a baritone and relies heavily on the middle voice.

Spinto Tenor Vocal Models

Francesco Tamagno (1850-1905) created the OTELLO of Verdi. It was said that his voice made the chandelier at La Scala rattle when he sang. Listen to his OTELLO recording, keeping in mind how and when it was made.

Ramón Vinay was a favorite of Toscanini and can be heard on an OTELLO recording with the great maestro. He had a great gift for the declamatory style, as did Mario Del Monaco who took on the challenge of OTELLO after Vinay.

Other *spinto* tenors to hear are Giovanni Martinelli (1885-1969), Giacomo Lauri-Volpi (1893-1978), and the American, Richard Tucker (1913-1975).

Some voices have the ability to sing many parts. This depends on the artistry, the skill, and the dramatic values the singer is capable of expressing. For instance, Franco Corelli (1921-2003) sang the more lyric roles as well as the *spinto* repertoire of ANDREA CHÉNIER, AÏDA, LA FANCIULLA DEL WEST, and IL TROVATORE. His voice was one of the most thrilling I have ever heard. His extensive range and command of the ability to diminish his voice were outstanding. He was as at home in the Meyerbeer opera LES HUGENOTS, with its great vocal extension, as he was as Calaf in TURANDOT. He retired early and, sadly, he died in 2003. He has a legacy of recordings, however.

Plácido Domingo is a remarkable singer in that he has sung operas from all repertoires from L'ELISIR D'AMORE, ROMÉO ET JULIETTE, and LA BOHÈME, to THE TALES OF HOFFMANN. He sings all the Verdi *spinto* roles—Calaf in TURANDOT, as did Corelli, and proceeding on to OTELLO, and finally the Wagnerian *heldentenor* roles.

I was present at Domingo's first performance of TURANDOT at the Arena di Verona in the 60s. He was very young and his Turandot was Birgit Nilsson. The critics praised him, but added that he would sing only a few years if he continued to sing such a heavy repertoire. This shows how often critics are wrong! He is a master of his own voice and surely has to be constant in striving to maintain it, with his schedule.

James McCracken (1926-1988) was the first American tenor to have great success in OTELLO as well as PAGLIACCI and Radames in AÏDA. He was a dear colleague of mine in our PAGLIACCI in The Philadelphia Opera.

The best known and possibly the most beloved tenor is, of course, Luciano Pavarotti. He is another singer who spans more than one voice type, singing both lyric and *spinto* tenor roles, but not the dramatic roles. He has sung for the same number of years as Domingo, and although he limits himself to recording the heavier parts, he certainly has captured the hearts of many who would not have otherwise been drawn to opera. He is an intuitive singer and really is not a musician *per se*, but his knowledge of his voice is phenomenal. It would be impossible to sing these roles over a period of 35 years and not have an involuntary technique

Dramatic Tenor James McCracken with author, backstage after PAGLIACCI in Philadelphia

based on the ear! At times, the more complicated the singer's technical approach becomes, the less likely he or she is able to freely express the music.

Sergej Larin is another example of a *spinto* tenor. He is Russian, but is very convincing in roles as varied as PAGLIACCI, FIDELIO, LA FORZA DEL DESTINO, and LOHENGRIN. He records for Arte Nova.

Two of the newer tenors in the field of the *spinto* are José Cura and Salvatore Licitra. Domingo is a champion of Cura, but I find his voice still needs schooling and he has great problems with his high voice. I heard him in Washington as OTELLO with Domingo conducting and he was forced to pull away from all the high notes in haste! For me, his voice is less interesting due to its over-dark, sometimes muddy sound, although the voice has great potential. But, I have heard him on Lyon recordings. By listening, you will determine whether you feel it is a natural sound and if its weightiness will bear the effects of time.

Licitra was flown in to substitute for Pavarotti when he was ill during a run of IL TROVATORE. While I am not very enthusiastic about his voice so far, he seems to have considerable audience appeal. He recently recorded IL TROVATORE with Barbara Frittoli.

Marcello Giordani is currently a very impressive tenor. He is a Sicilian, like Di Stefano. He began as a more lyric tenor, but evolved into heavier roles. He was wonderful in Bellini's IL PIRATA at the Metropolitan. He has a very fine extended range and is now preparing a more *spinto* repertoire.

I have recently discovered two young tenors who do not fit the mold of the opera singer and yet they both have voices which suggest that they might have possibilities to become two of the NEW TENORS (after Pavarotti and Domingo). The first is Mario Frangoulis, a young man of Greek heritage. He studied with the famous tenor, Alfredo Kraus, but has also developed a style of singing that is contemporary Italian popular music. His range is extensive, and on his CD he combines a popular ballad with the aria "E Lucevan le Stelle" from Puccini's TOSCA. The effect is startling yet very convincing. He maintains a classical technique which he uses in the aria, and then returns to the ballad mode.

The other tenor is Alessandro Safina, an Italian from Siena. There is no biography on his CD, but his voice is quite beautiful. He begins with the aria from PHANTOM OF THE OPERA and finishes in a key which demonstrates his operatic range. The other selections on the CD are unfamiliar to me, but I was very pleased to know that there are real voices singing popular music. The appeal of this could easily draw younger audiences to a more classical taste in music.

The Baritones—Lyric and Verdi

A Description of the Baritone Voice

Although not formally specified, the baritone voice is generally of two types. The first is a more lyric baritone sound suited to the young leads in opera. It requires ease in the *tessitura*, which goes to a low G or an A flat in the bass clef. The color is lighter and lends itself to lighter roles.

The second type is the Verdi baritone. It has a heavier and darker quality. This does not mean a thick or wooly sound; the core of the sound must always remain slender in order to make full use of the resonances.

In between the baritone and bass voices is yet another class, the bass-baritone. The bass-baritone is able to encompass both heavier baritone roles as well as some bass roles, depending on the weight and the range of the voice. The range varies, but it extends from a low F in the bass clef to an F in the G clef.

Roles for the Baritone

The lighter and more lyrical baritone voice is suited to the works of Mozart and Handel, as well as the lighter roles of Puccini, such as Marcello or Schaunard in LA BOHÈME. Rossini's Il BARBIERE DI SIVIGLIA and Silvio in I PAGLIACCI are also of the more lyric baritone repertoire. These voices also can be ideal for lieder repertoire.

The heavier baritone repertoire encompasses the Verdi operas as well as *verismo* operas, such as Carlo Gérard in ANDREA CHÉNIER,

Scarpia in TOSCA, and Barnaba in LA GIOCONDA.

The roles of Blitch in Carlisle Floyd's SUSANNAH and the role of MEFISTOFELE of Boito are examples of roles for the bass-baritone.

Baritone Vocal Models

Two examples of the lyric baritone voice are Thomas Hampson and Gino Quilico. Dwayne Croft is also an outstanding young baritone who is developing into a more dramatic singer with a heavier sound allowing him to sing bigger roles. Hampson is also essaying a heavier repertoire, but for me, he is much more successful in lieder.

While I was in Italy I studied with a man who exemplified the style of the true Verdi baritone. His name is Carlo Tagliabue (1898-1978) and his recital of arias is worth having. They have been released on the Preiser label. He was greatly esteemed at La Scala.

Among the earlier Verdi baritones was Titta Ruffo (1877-1953), a contemporary of Caruso.

More recent baritones of this type are the late Ettore Bastianini (1922-1967), Piero Cappuccilli, and Renato Bruson. These men have sung all the heaviest Verdi and Puccini roles. Cappuccilli can be heard on many complete operas as well as in a stunning video performance from La Scala as Michele in Puccini's IL TABARRO. Bruson can be seen in a fine performance of MACBETH on video, made in the 90s in Vienna.

I must add the names of several great Americans who were very successful in the heavy baritone roles: Robert Merrill, Cornell MacNeil, and Leonard Warren, as well as the fine Lawrence Tibbett and Sherill Milnes.

The young Dimitri Hvorostovsky is another example of this type of baritone. He has a wonderful instrument but it often seems unnaturally dark, perhaps due to his being Russian.

Norman Treigle (1927-1975) was the ideal singer for the bass-baritone roles. I made my debut with Treigle in LE NOZZE DI FIGARO, singing the Countess to his Figaro.

Samuel Ramey is the most famous for these roles at the moment. He has sung the bel canto roles of Rossini as well as the heavier roles of Verdi and Boito's MEFISTOFELE. George London (1920-1985) was an exemplary artist of this repertoire. An Italian bass-baritone of note was Giuseppe Taddei. He was a consummate artist and excelled in Mozart as well as in baritone roles such as Germont in Verdi's LA TRAVIATA and in the title role of FALSTAFF.

Both Ruggero Raimondi and James Morris have sung parts that can be called either baritone or *basso-cantante*. Mozart's DON GIOVANNI has been sung by Ezio Pinza and Cesare Siepi, both called basses, but of this more lyric type. Nicolai Ghiaurov has sung both the DON GIOVANNI as well as MEFISTOFELE, but also the pure bass roles in DON CARLO, ERNANI, etc.

The young Bryn Terfel has a remarkable sound for the bass-baritone repertoire, but he is now beginning to eye all the Wagnerian parts, and I hope his voice will not suffer. (See additional notes below.) Terfel is equally at home with the lighter music of Broadway. The naturalness with which he sings this music reveals much about his technique.

This book would be incomplete without acknowledging a very special singer, Richard Rovin, who came to me in his forties with a lifelong desire to sing opera. He had been successful in the business world but never felt satisfied with his life. I must admit I was sympathetic with his ambition, but I was frankly doubtful he could realize his dream. He lacked musical skills as well as a background in languages, and found their pronunciation very difficult.

But it turned out that Richard had amazing dedication and he pursued every avenue in order to improve. After a rather brief period of study with me, he traveled to Italy for a summer course with Gianni Raimondi, a former colleague of mine. Richard sang his first role as Amonasro in AÏDA onstage in Slovakia, followed by several performances in TRAVIATA as Germont. The latter was his favorite role and he performed it in the US, as he did editions of MADAMA BUTTERFLY, the Console, and TOSCA (in the role of Scarpia). He was contracted to sing in Bologna in Jerome Hines' opera, I AM THE WAY, and also his dream role, RIGOLETTO.

Richard Rovin

Then, as unexpectedly as he came into my life, Richard died suddenly from an unexplainable illness. I shall always value having worked with him for several years and seeing him become a true Verdi baritone. His dear wife, Elaine, is blessed to have many live recordings of his voice. I am sure he is still blessing all who hear him.

I have made many live recordings of Richard. Two are included on the enclosed DVD: "Largo al factotum," in an onstage performance of IL BARBIERE DI SIVIGLIA; and "Di provenza il mar il sol," from LA TRAVIATA. Another is included on the enclosed CD, singing "Nemico della patria" from ANDREA CHÉNIER.

Additional Comments for the Baritone

Singers like Bryn Terfel, who has a remarkable sound for the bass-baritone repertoire, would best stay away from the Wagnerian parts, or their voices could suffer as did James Morris's voice. The Wagner repertoire may be artistically rewarding, but the vocal demands to be heard over the orchestra in a house like the Metropolitan often cause the voice to become wooden, and a slow wobble develops.

The Basso-Cantante and Bass

A Description of the Basso-Cantante and Bass Voices

The last category is the bass voice. It is the darkest of the men's voices in color and lends itself to serious parts. The basses in the bel canto repertoire are required to have much agility. They are often the more comic roles. (I have included vocalises and comments from Luigi Lablache, the bass that created many parts in Bellini's operas as well as those of Donizetti. These can be found in the section of vocalises.)

Bass Orival Bento-Gonçalves as Banquo in Teatro da Paz Belem production of MACBETH

The *basso-cantante* is a more lyrical bass, which is wonderful in Mozart roles. See also the comments in the baritone section.

Roles for the Basso-Cantante and Bass

The dark quality of this voice lends itself to the most serious parts, such as the King and the Inquisitor in Verdi's DON CARLO, as well as Oroveso in Bellini's NORMA, Padre Guardiano in LA FORZA DEL DESTINO of Verdi, Silva in ERNANI, also by Verdi, and of course BORIS GODUNOV of Mussorgsky.

But the uncommon or unexpected deepness of the voice can also give it a comic air. The *buffo* or comic bass sings many parts in Rossini's operas. *Buffo* roles also include Dulcamara in L'ELISIR D'AMORE of

Donizetti, Bartolo in Mozart's LE NOZZE DI FIGARO, and Don Basilio and Bartolo in IL BARBIERE DI SIVIGLIA.

Of the more lyrical bass roles, there are Leporello in Mozart's DON GIOVANNI, while Boito's MEFISTOFELE is dramatic. (See also the discussion of the bass-baritone roles in the baritone section.)

Basso-Cantante and Bass Vocal Models

The Russians are noted for their bass voices. One of the most renowned was the remarkable actor-singer Fyodor Chaliapin (1873 - 1938). He was famous in the part of BORIS GODUNOV and as Prince Galitsky in PRINCE IGOR. Another voice of this type was Alexander Kipnis (1891 - 1978), who can be heard in a recent release of arias and lieder. More recently, two great bass voices are those of Nicola Rossi-Lemeni and Boris Christoff. I sang in a season with Christoff and I was always in awe of his magnificent voice and stage presence. He would seem to me to be the closest in style and voice to Chaliapin.

Bass Paolo Montarsolo backstage after COSÌ FAN TUTTE in Trieste

My favorite colleague in this repertoire was Paolo Montarsolo. I sang Fiordiligi to his Don Alfonso in COSÌ FAN TUTTE. He was a superb singer of comic, *buffo* roles.

The following more lyrical basses are also discussed in the baritone section: Both Ruggero Raimondi and James Morris have sung *basso-cantante* roles. Nicolai Ghiaurov has sung both the DON GIOVANNI as well as MEFISTOFELE, but also the pure bass roles in DON CARLO,

ERNANI, etc. Ezio Pinza and Cesare Siepi also have this repertoire.

Of the singers who sang the bass-baritone roles, listen to Norman Treigle, Samuel Ramey, George London, and Giuseppe Taddei.

I close this section with a tribute to two great basses: Nicolai Ghiaurov (also discussed in the baritone section) and the American, Jerome Hines. Both have had illustrious careers. Ghiaurov was unforgettable as DON GIOVANNI in the Salzburg Festival. His other roles in MEFISTOFELE, FAUST, and DON CARLO were unique for their beauty of sound, as well as his characterizations. This great artist died on March 6th, 2004. Jerome Hines enjoyed many years as a leading bass at the Metropolitan in the same repertoire. He passed away in 2003. In addition to being a marvelous bass, Jerome Hines was a composer and writer. His book *Great Singers on Great Singing* is a classic,[*] and his last book was *The Four Voices of Man*.[†]

---

[*] Jerome Hines, *Great Singers on Great Singing* (New York: Proscenium Publishers, Inc., 1994).

[†] —————, *The Four Voices of Man* (New York: Proscenium Publishers, Inc., 1997).

Part 5

The Professional Singer

**The author in front of a poster for her
New York City Tully Hall recital.**

Preparing for a Role

Your Repertoire

To choose your repertoire, you must have a clear idea of your voice and its potential. The previous section on voice types will help you, as will your teacher and, above all, your own ear.

Studying arias for competitions is only a very small part of your work. When you have advanced to the stage of role study, it should be *ongoing*.

If you are serious about an opera career, *do not wait* for contracts before studying roles that are ideal for your voice. It takes time to "grow" into a role, and the discipline of working is hard to recover if you are not in *allenamento*, or vocal form. Your technique will be challenged to develop as you call on it to achieve your ideals.

Experiment with a role that you know will be in your vocal future. It will help you grow. Many times I have been aware that singers have only concentrated on the arias and have given little time or thought to the whole role, much less the background and the characterization. What is your current repertoire? How many roles could you sing on short notice if you had the chance to substitute for an indisposed singer?

Who does not aspire to occupy the first place in his field already is beginning to give in to become second, and little by little, he is content to be last.
Trans. Tosi

In answer to my one and only fan letter, Kirsten Flagstad advised me that singing involves "a lifetime of study." If her statement doesn't appeal to you, and if you don't enjoy study and the process itself, you should realistically evaluate your career goals. It *is* a day-to-day process and sometimes it is difficult to be convinced you are making improvements. My advice is to keep on keeping on!

Studying a Role

Who studies searches for the best, whether it be in the style of fifteen or twenty years ago or today: because the good as well as the bad is from all times: we must expect to find all, understand it, and profit from it.

Trans. Tosi

The Italians say the best way to study is to study twenty minutes for every ten minutes you sing. This is good, general advice, but I would add that your method of study is as important as the time you spend, if not more so.

Preparing a role means to learn the text apart from the music. Observe the score from the point of its musical drama, and slowly learn all the notes and rhythms independently from the text. Gain an understanding of what the words and music are communicating so that you can put feeling into your interpretation. Remember that every sound you will be singing, even in rehearsal, must give life to the emotions behind the words, or else your role will never come to life onstage.

After this study, when you put the text and music together, you will not have learned "mistakes" that are hard to correct, and your voice will not have been exhausted during your preparatory work.

One of my teachers in Italy taught me to work on a role in the following way. It is a thorough method that will allow you to efficiently proceed through the most difficult works:

1. First, translate the text, word for word, to learn its meaning.

2. Next, study the music, giving your keen attention to all the rhythms, BUT without singing! Look at all the phrases, pronunciations, and the ideal breaths to let them flow. This includes vowel modification, as I have explained earlier. You may declaim the text to learn the words, rhythm, and breathing, but again, do not sing.

3. After the preliminary work, sing through the first act of the opera. I have found this to be a much more thorough way of studying than to sing at a role on first sight.

4. With a good coach or accompanist who can give you additional guidance on phrasing and diction, study one act at a time for three consecutive sessions. After that, continue on in the same manner for the other acts.

5. At the end of those sessions and in the following week, sing through the entire opera in one sitting. Work on the more difficult sections as part of your vocalizing.

6. After a couple of days of vocal rest, repeat the entire opera as before.

7. If you do not have a contract to sing in the near future, put that opera aside and begin to study another one.

Learning a variety of suitable roles, with the kind of preparation outlined above, can give you unexpected opportunities in case of an immediate need to substitute for another singer who is indisposed.

Further Notes on Role Preparation

Visualization, **imagery**, and **imagination** are the tools of the true artist. Use them to become mentally aware of what you deem beautiful, and the kind of sound and the effect you desire.

A gesture is only as good as the expression on your face that accompanies it. If you are concerned with "tone" and not "meaning," you cannot make true movements or gestures.

Perform with ease. Singers often equate tension with feelings, but if you can perform any music with great ease, it tends to be convincing on that basis alone. The music is the performer's primary creative contribution. The words and the music are the meaning, regardless of the singer's actual thought process.

Chado—A metaphor. Chado is a century-old Japanese tea ceremony. There are 331 distinct steps which, when performed properly, create an overall sense of grace and elegance. The principles of Chado are *harmony, purity, respect, poise, tranquility,* and *integrity*. Chado is a wonderful metaphor for the beauty and harmony the artist can create with the proper preparation and care.

The Day of the Performance

I suggest vocalizing very little on the day of the performance. You already will have had sufficient rehearsals to solve any vocal considerations, and the tendency is to overdo singing because of the anticipation. I've heard Italians who are big stars say they like to "warm up" onstage. Of course, you also hear about the great Wagnerian singer, Lilli Lehmann, who took an hour to do her great scale! (Lehmann's Great Scale is presented in the Vocalise section of this book; but I do not advise warming up with the Great Scale on the day of a performance.)

Voice Rescue

Stage Fright

Every performer is sometimes plagued with stage fright. The question is how to overcome this state, which robs us of our ease and ability to communicate through our singing. There are several methods for reducing stage fright. This is not to say that these will eliminate the condition completely, but they will enable you to release tension and free your voice to be more expressive.

Be Prepared

The first important step is preparation. Without a concentrated effort to learn the music and text perfectly, there can be little security in performance.

Problems with memory of the text come from not knowing the exact meaning (not the approximate meaning) of every word you sing.

The clear knowledge of rhythm, tempo, coronas, and phrase dynamics are all vital to true preparation. These become one entity when properly prepared. The unprepared singer usually concentrates only on the sound for itself, without any relation to the music. He is preoccupied only with the climactic high notes and is usually fearful of the end of the aria. It all comes down to focus.

Study your errors well. Oh, what a great lesson! They cost little, teach much. From what we learn the most ignorant fault becomes the greatest teacher.
Trans. Tosi

We may also speak of that most important state: readiness. Pavarotti says that you must be sure of the pitch and the sound at the instant before you sing. This means mental readiness, not physical stiffness.

Focus on What You Are Communicating Musically, Not on Yourself

Any fear about being sure of your music is bound to attack your breathing first, leading to fear of long phrases, and manipulating the throat to conserve the air. If your attention is on the breath, it cannot be on the tone, and if the text has not become an integral part of the music itself, your attention will be divided in several directions. The result: you will be in a perpetual state of fear and your creative juices will be frozen.

I had the good fortune to attend a weekend workshop with the late Eloise Ristad, author of *A Soprano on Her Head.** It is an invaluable book for singers. Eloise worked with all kinds of performers, helping them to overcome their blocks to performance. Her keen imagination and love of music gave her the insights to encourage performers to approach their work in many ways. Focusing on one thing at a time was all-important. To practice this, Eloise encouraged all of us to learn juggling. It involves vision, rhythm, and coordination all in one.

Eloise gave us a script for an imaginary audition. I was the chosen "guinea pig." Several of the other participants were to act as judges in a mock audition. When I entered they acted very cold and disinterested. They asked what I would sing, and when I said VISSI D' ARTE, they cringed and informed me that they had already heard that aria many times and furthermore, they had very limited time.

I had sung for years in Europe and certainly did not feel fear—or so I thought. My first feeling was anger, then stiffness and a need to win their approval. What I did was acceptable, if uninspired. I felt a lack of focus.

If I have any message to the young singer, it would be: stick to your work and study systematically, wholeheartedly. If you do not love your work enough to give it your best thought, to make sacrifices for it, there is something wrong with you. Then choose some other line of work, to which you can give undivided attention and love.

Geraldine Farrar -
Etude Magazine
interview

* Eloise Ristad, *A Soprano on Her Head* (Moab, UT: Real People Press, 1982).

Afterwards, Eloise explained how I had let the critic take over in me and "run the show." We then repeated the exercise, but this time she told me to see the judges only as receptive to my singing, to be aware of the joy I derive from it, and lastly, to direct my full attention to the balls of my feet all the while. That single focus wiped out all the nerves, and I felt completely in control of my voice and the situation. If such a simple idea could change my perspective that much, I could see the great value in clear mental direction.

I do not mean to say that thinking of the balls of your feet will solve all your problems of stage fright, but it does indicate the value of "one-pointed" mental focus.

Come From a Place of Power

The outward desire to please, to read the faces of the judges, to, in essence, plead for acceptance, is all coming from a place of fear and insecurity. If you sing, you sing for love of the music, and the desire to communicate this—to express joy at the opportunity to sing—will allow you to come from a place of power, which will bring good results.

The fear of not being perfect is perhaps the greatest cause of stage fright. It freezes the life out of your performance. How often have you read about performances that were vocally acceptable, but cold and uninteresting? We communicate through our "humanness." If our "critic" starts asserting himself—judges and tries to control—we become tense, stilted, and ultimately undervalued.

Dear Boris Goldovsky once said, "Young singers all try to compete with the greatest qualities in all current singers. They want the high notes of this singer, the agility of that one, and the vocal power of another…Try being yourself. And this means alive and human…not dead. The dead are embalmed…they have no warmth, although their skin appears to be perfect, without blemishes."

We can ask if the voice itself is the most important element to become a good singer. Although such a question can seem ridiculous and absurd, for our part we affirm that intelligence is important, if not more important than the instrument itself. In fact, a small voice, if perfectly trained and used with ingenuity, can give much artistic pleasure. On the other hand, an ample voice with more beauty, if lacking in intelligence, will never produce the same result and will make us sad that such a gift is wasted.

Trans. V. Ricci

*Every artist dips
his brush into his
own soul and
paints his own
nature into his
pictures.*

Henry Ward Beecher

I like to think of it as vulnerability, or being human. Callas, with all her tremendous gifts, was a perfectionist—to her own detriment in the end. Her standards were of such a demand for perfection that she could not abide any less given by others. She demanded the ultimate from herself at all times, and when she could no longer meet her own standards, she began to lose her confidence. I attended her last performance of MEDÉA at La Scala. It was a tragedy to see the great singer in such distress.

In her Juilliard Master Classes, Callas was sometimes severe, but she was attempting to stir something in each singer...to inspire them to be more. One day Callas said to a young singer, "Whatever you do, never be coy or cute." She shared much invaluable information. She often demonstrated phrases that were magnificent. I shall never forget her singing part of the final phrases of the Judgment scene of Amneris for an aspiring mezzo. Her desire to communicate overcame her own fear, which was at its height in that period. I heard this from the unique coach, Alberta Masiello, of the Metropolitan Opera. I was coaching with her at that time.

Did some of the great singers often have doubts about their voices? Corelli never stopped doubting himself and was always asking people if he were singing acceptably. A brilliant coach, with whom I had the great good fortune to work with, told me that in Callas' later years, that is, in the period of the Master Classes at Juilliard, she studied every day. Her voice still retained its power at times, but her nerve and faith in herself were gone.

To recap the subject of stage fright, the main concern is attitude. If the "inner critic" asserts itself, we have two possibilities: either refocus on your intentions for the performance of the music for itself, or agree to diminish your self-worth by concentrating only on "How am I doing?" It is your choice! Become a vocal painter. Color the music with your true emotions, your humanity, your vulnerability. Then you will captivate your audience and free your voice to sing!

Vocal Health

I am often asked about the subject of vocal health. For me, the principle consideration is to take preventative measures. Here are my suggestions, based on many years of experience with my own vocal health and that of my students and fellow singers.

Cold and Drafts

It may seem quaint today to be concerned about cold weather and drafts because we are so used to the idea that we can take a pill to ward off any problems. But this is not true, and it is especially not true for singers! Pay attention to the weather predictions and dress accordingly. The Scarf is a critical article of clothing for a singer. Indoors, it will protect your neck and back if you are caught unawares in a draft or in air conditioning. Outdoors it will protect your neck and back from cold and wind, or if the weather suddenly changes. Always keep a scarf with you. (You almost never see Pavarotti without a scarf around his neck!)

Cold Air: A sudden burst of cold air can cause hoarseness.

Talking in Cold Air: Don't talk when you are in the cold outdoor air. Italians often hold a scarf over their mouths at such a time.

Drafts: Stay aware of drafts on your back and neck, even if you are wearing a scarf.

Care of Throat and Mouth

Screaming: This might seem obvious, but it bears emphasizing: Screaming at sports events, and the like, can irritate your vocal cords and make it difficult to sing the next day. Save screaming for emergencies.

Straining the Voice: Do not be tempted to push your voice beyond its natural size for vocal effects. For instance, some sopranos compensate for dramatic outbursts by forcing their lowest sounds into a harsh, open chest sound. If the voice is produced correctly, it carries over the orchestra, not through it.

Gargling: ALCOLOL (NO! Not alcohol!) is very good for gargling. You can also make your own remedy with a half teaspoon of lemon juice, a tablespoon or two of honey, eight ounces of warm water, and a pinch of baking soda.

Dental and Oral Health: Much research has been done on the connection between oral health and bodily health. The mouth is the main opening to our body, where we receive not only our sustenance, but many undesirable invaders, as well. It is essential to keep teeth and gums clean, and free of bacterial sources such as old fillings. Practice good oral hygiene and visit your dentist regularly to avoid problems in the mouth that could interfere with your singing.

One major point: Never put your hands or fingers in your mouth. Hands are a major source of infection. Be conscious of this: don't pull off your gloves with your teeth, or lick your fingers (eating, turning pages, etc.). Wash your hands before eating, especially when eating things with your hands, such as bread.

Healthy Elimination

Another health consideration is healthy "elimination." Italians very often take old fashioned castor oil several days before a performance. I can attest that it does seem to clarify the sound of the voice and in turn improves resonance. I also believe in an occasional colonic irrigation, but this is a controversial subject for many in the medical profession.

The All-Important Neti Pot

The Neti Pot is an indispensable tool for singers. What is it? It is a small pitcher widely used in India, in the Yogic tradition. It enables you to wash out, irrigate, and moisten your nasal passages and sinuses by pouring salt water into the nostrils. The Neti Pot pictured in the photo is porcelain; it looks like a magic lantern—and is almost as helpful!

To use the Neti Pot: Simply mix lukewarm water and about a half teaspoon of salt in the Neti Pot, to make a saline solution. Taste-test the water to make sure it is the right temperature and has the desired amount of salinity. Pour the salt water, for several seconds, into one nostril. The salt water flows through your sinuses, and comes out the other nostril. Then stop and blow your nose. Repeat this until you've emptied the pot, switching occasionally to the other nostril. This may sound ghastly to you, but please try it; it is soothing, and very effective.

The Neti Pot has many uses, all extremely important to the singer: It is used for general nasal congestion, sinus dryness, sinusitis, colds, nasal blockages, allergies, hayfever, general breathing difficulties, snoring, and more.

Porcelain Neti Pot

There are various types of Neti Pots, including porcelain and stainless steel. They are inexpensive, and you can buy them from natural product outlets. (There are several web sites devoted to the product.)

If you are ever in a pinch and without a Neti Pot, you can try "sniffling in" salt water, although this might take some practice.

Symptoms of Concern to Singers

Sore Throat: Purchase a small portable steamer and use it with a teaspoon or two of ALCOLOL (NO! Not alcohol!) It can be ordered by your pharmacist if you can not find it easily.

Nasal Congestion: For general nasal congestion I recommend using the Neti Pot, discussed above, rather than decongestants and other drugs.

Coughing: If it is constant, coughing may be a sign of an infection, or it can be dehydration due to the lack of water or the lack of humidity in the air. The ideal humidity should be 65 percent, according to one famous throat specialist.

Colds: If you feel a cold coming on, drink lots of water and take a holistic capsule called Echinacea three times a day, and also a couple of packets of EMERGEN-C from your health food store. And of course, take citrus juice and vitamins.

Allergies: I cannot address allergies because they may require medical advice, but I am not generally in favor of courses of antibiotics or steroid injections. They should be used only if all else fails and you MUST sing an important performance. However, many people have reported a big reduction in allergic reactions to airborne pollens and the like, with regular cleansing of the sinuses using a Neti Pot (see above).

Tightness in the Lungs: Caffeine can cause a tightness of the lungs in certain individuals, affecting the ease of breath. If you have a hard time relaxing your lungs or getting a naturally full breath, experiment with eliminating caffeine from your diet.

Throat Clearing: Throat clearing is often caused by sinus drainage, or mucus (see below). The Neti Pot helps reduce the need for throat clearing.

Mucus: Dairy products can affect the lungs and throat of some people, causing a thick feeling in the lungs and mucus formation. If you have this problem, experiment with eliminating dairy from your diet.

Rest

The energy and concentration required for singing demanding music takes its toll on the body. I suggest an additional nap in the afternoon after lunch and before the evening rehearsal, if your schedule permits and you are singing in a theater with this schedule. This is customary in European theaters. It certainly is a "must" for all the Italians with whom I have sung!

A Caution about Drugs

Antihistamines: Antihistamines dry the throat! For this reason I am not a believer in their use for singers. There are also other problems associated with their use, and I urge you to research alternative, natural ways to deal with colds and allergies.

In fact, many drugs have side effects that can affect the voice, either directly or indirectly. Lithium is another drug that dries the throat, as well as the mouth. Some of the side-effects of drugs can be long-lasting and very damaging. The singer needs to be vigilant about being fully informed of the side effects of the drugs he or she is taking, both prescription and over-the-counter!

I urge you to research natural alternatives. Instead of popping a pill to mask a symptom, find out what is causing the problem (lack of a certain nutrient? lack of sleep or exercise? need for sinus irrigation?) and address it appropriately.

A Career in Singing

The challenges to arriving at a successful career in opera and other types of singing seem almost impossible to many singers
because of technical problems, a fear of high
notes, lack of projection and, most importantly, not knowing how to express music
unhampered by technical preoccupation. In
the previous sections of this book you will
have learned how to address these problems.
In this chapter I will pass along wisdom of a
different sort: the many "ins and outs" of
building a singing career in a changing world.

Baritone Ugo Savarese, center, and the
author, right, onstage in COSÌ FAN TUTTE,
Teatro Bellini, Catania, Sicily.

Building a Successful Singing Career

First of all, you must be gifted with a voice that can be molded and
developed, and you must have "honed" your musical skills. Most of this
book addresses this aspect of career building, and it is of course the
most important thing. But there is more you can do for yourself, or you
will never get noticed!

A second important requirement is that you address your "packaging." In today's market, this consists of attention to dress, weight, and "all over" appearance. This is due to the visual presentation of concerts and operas, frequently to the very large audiences of television and film. (Still, if you are a Pavarotti, a Sutherland, a Ben Heppner, or a Jessye Norman, it won't matter!)

Third, assess your strongest points in singing and choose your audition arias to put them in the foreground. Of course, you will have already built up an appropriate repertoire.

What are the qualities of a great performer? Art, not artifice. Simplicity. Joy and Commitment.

Fourth, keep current on news in the business. Subscribe to music journals such as *The Classical Singer*, *Opera News*, and *Opera America*. There you will find all the news on competitions and auditions for apprentice programs, study, summer programs, and auditions for opera companies. These publications also contain helpful articles and insights from professionals. There are also many sites on the Internet that give vital information about the market.

Fifth, if you are still at an age to compete, by all means get the experience of competitions. Ask for "feed-back" in any case. The comments you receive will be very revealing on where you are vocally and where you need to concentrate your efforts.

Sixth, be sure of your stage demeanor. How do you enter the stage? What is your body language? Is it positive? Energized? Fearful? Hesitating? Do you establish rapport with your accompanist? In your first eye contact with those hearing you, do you give the impression that you are happy to be there and that you love what you are singing?

Seventh, be realistic about your prospects for a career. If you have questions, ask a qualified musician in the field to advise you.

These suggestions are not meant to discourage you—only to give you a clearer idea of your career challenges. The real adversary to your progress is your "inner critic." It parades as discouragement, self-criticism, statistics, your "true" value, your age, comments from well-meaning authorities (and maybe not). Once you allow in this kind of thinking, your creative energy is sapped and you have a vocal "fall-out."

In your study of singing, never start over. Savor the good things you have learned and build on them.

There is no "quick fix" for acquiring the necessary skills for a singing career. It requires dedication, courage, and cultivating JOY in the process while keeping the goal always in mind.

The Seven Qualities of an Outstanding Singer

I have noticed the following qualities in singers who stand above the others:

Clarity of intention to succeed and the "follow-through" that makes it a reality.

> There is a word in Italian that you may not know. It is *la grinta*. It is hard to translate, but it is used in the case of an athlete who aspires to win a race. He is tireless in his decision to overcome all obstacles. The singer with *la grinta* keeps the goal always in view.

Optimism.

> The outstanding singer has the ability to surmount many obstacles and find ways to turn them into "positives."

Dedication to the highest ideals of artistic expression.

> The outstanding singer understands that it is not enough to know the translation of every word of the text, and goes a

Let me give you one of my great secrets. Never give the public all you have. That is, the singer owes it to herself never to go beyond the boundaries of her vocal possibilities. The singer who sings to the utmost every time is like the athlete who exhausts himself to the state of collapse. This is the only way in which I can account for what critics term "the remarkable preservation" of my own voice.
Dame Nellie Melba

step further, digging into the background and the composer's conception of the work.

The skill to become one with the content of the aria or song.

The outstanding singer makes it real to her by summoning up feelings that she has experienced in her own life. Lotte Lehmann encouraged me to make up a story or remember an incident when I felt a strong emotion, and then transfer it into the music. In this way, the singer succeeds in taking music off the page and making it meaningful, instead of a vocal, technical display.

It is not because things are difficult that we do not dare; it is because we do not dare that they are difficult.

Seneca

The ability to keenly evaluate how to market his particular voice and talent, to choose a repertoire that shows him at his best, and to know where he fits in.

In the play "Master Class" by Terence McNally about the Callas Master Classes at Juilliard, Callas admonishes a singer for not having a "look." This is important. Call it "putting your best foot forward." Are you convincing in your demeanor and do you convey the assurance to convince your audience or those who hear you in auditions that you are thoroughly prepared and ready to perform?

A willingness to take risks in order to get experience.

This does not mean attempting a role in a big house that will ultimately harm your voice. A secondary role in a company with important singers can assure you that you will be heard by many scouts and managers who attend these performances. There is a quotation from the Bible that has proved to be true time and time again. It is Proverbs 18:16: "A man's gifts make room for him and bring him before great men."

An outstanding image, both in the visual and vocal sense.

Imagery plays as big a part in singing as it does in life. If you do not dare to raise your sights above and beyond our everyday expectancies, it is impossible to realize your full potential. However, if your only reason for having a ringing high C is to hear the applause, you may miss many of the pleasures of communicating music. Most great singers' voices are remembered for their color, style, and serious commitment to the music and its beauty, and only occasionally for their high C!

Artists must be sacrificed to their art. Like bees, they must put their lives into the sting they give.

Ralph Waldo Emerson

With the above thoughts in mind, I urge you to write a questionnaire for yourself evaluating your realistic possibilities. Is it your dream to get a contract at the Met? They are interested in how much experience you have had and in what roles, where you have performed them, and of course your age and musical training. This questionnaire is not to discourage you from pursuing your dreams, but it is a tool to help you become realistic about your possibilities and to show you what you need to work on. And remember, there are always exceptions to the rules and you may be hired on your very first audition. Always audition with the intention of being hired!

And if you are convinced you were born to be there on the stage with the best…don't allow anyone to deter you from trying.

The Proactive Approach

Stephen Covey, in his book on highly motivated people,* speaks about the three central values he leaned from the work of Victor Frankl:

The experiential — that which happens to us (passive)

The creative — that which we bring forth (initiative)

The attitudinal — how we respond to circumstances (reactive)

All three of these modes of behavior have their place, and are appropriate at various times. However, of the three, I have come to believe that the second, what we create in life, is the most important. Taking responsibility for your career is the most important step. It means action, not "waiting to be discovered" or "responding to another's vision."

Imagination and conscience are two valuable tools for self-discovery and expanding your career horizons. Through imagination you visualize your creative potential, and through conscience you can find ways to implement and develop your talents.

Be "opportunity minded," not "problem minded." Balance in life and balance in singing go hand in hand. Outline the parameters of your study, that is, what and by what date. Challenge yourself! Setting mini goals for yourself can help you keep up the momentum. Pick up all your current arias and re-study them as if they were new to you. Experiment with the phrases. Find new colors in your voice through your feelings.

If you are drawn to the concert stage, seek out an opportunity to give a solo concert. Plan your program and set a date. Your creative juices will rush to help you. Or put together an evening of operatic excerpts. I found this a wonderful experience when I returned from Europe. I called the evening "An Operatic Odyssey." I sang excerpts from all my favorite

Go confidently in the direction of your dreams.

Henry David Thoreau

* Stephen R. Covey, *The 7 Habits of Highly Successful People* (New York: Simon and Schuster, 1990).

roles. I also wrote a commentary that was used as a "voice-over" during the semi-staged performance. These ventures keep your imagination and your creative instincts alive.

In closing, I think a career in singing comes down to finding your peace and your focus, through whatever means you adopt. Having a clear sense of your purpose and knowing why you want to sing is the key.

Glossary of Italian Terms

A fior di labbra	the sound heard as if "on the lips"
A piacere tempo	at the discretion of the singer
A piena voce	in full voice
Abellimento	embellished
Accelerando	increasing in speed
Accentato	accented
Allenamento	in vocal form
Andamento	tempo and movement
Appoggiato	leaned upon
Appoggio	the initiation of the sound
Armonici	the harmonics of a sound
Arpeggio	a chord whose notes are played in quick or slow succession
Aspro	bitter, penetrating
Basso-cantante	a more lyric bass with a range closer to a baritone
Brio	spirited, lively
Brunito	penetrating
Cabaletta	a fast, brilliant piece following a slower cavatina
Cadenza	the florid, brilliant ending to an aria

Cantabile	a slow, lyrical piece, or style of singing
Cavatina	a piece in the slow movement of the cantabile
Chiarezza	with clarity
Chiarezza di dizione	clarity of diction
Chiaro	clear
Chiaro-scuro	the dark-light sound in true Italian sounds
Corona	a sign meaning to hold the note longer; same as fermata
Declamato	the declaimed manner used in dramatic aria or recitatives
Duri	hard
Duttile	smooth, pliable, sweet
Espressivo	expressive
Fermata	a sign meaning to hold the note, as in a cadenza
Filare	to diminish, as in the messa di voce
Filo di voce	a thread of sound
Fioritura	like a flower…an ornamented passage
Forza	force, meaning forcefully sung
Frasseggio	manner of phrasing
Glissando	sliding
Grazia	grace
Incalzando	pressing, increasing speed
Ingrossando il suono	making the sound thicker
L'accento incisivo	an incisive accent
L'accento tagliente	a cutting accent
La grinta	determination, zeal
Legato	binding sounds together
Leggiero	lightly
Limpidezza	limpidity in the sound

Lirico	lyric
Martellato	a crisp attack of the sound (un martello means a hammer)
Messa di voce	increasing, then decreasing, the volume in a note
Mezza-voce	half voice
Morbidezza	tender or softness (as in tone-quality)
Morbido	soft
Mordenti	biting
Morendo	dying away
Mosso	moving quicker
Parlato	spoken (recitatives must approach this style)
Passaggio	zones of the voice between low, medium, and high
Pastosi	soft, fluid (like pasta)
Piano	soft
Poco (poco a poco)	little by little
Portamento	carrying the sound
Recita dal vivo	a live performance
Rinforzando	reinforcing
Rubato	the give and take in the tempo (robbed)
Secco	dry
Sfolgorante	released to high emotional energy ("una voce sfolgorante")
Sfumatura	a delicate diminishment of sound like disappearing smoke
Sopra-acuti	the extreme high notes (above high C) attributed to sopranos and tenors
Sostenuto	sustained
Sotto voce	quietly, an aside
Spinto	pushed (but refers to a lyric sound used dramatically)
Squillo	clarity and brilliance in sound

Stringendo	quickening of the tempo, gradually
Suoni luminosi	luminous sounds
Suono fisso	a tone lacking life and vibration
Suono timbrato	a tone with good timbre and "center"
Tempo primo	the original tempo after another has taken place
Tenebrosi	dark, without light
Tenuto	held, as in a cadenza
Tessitura	the approximate extension of range of a piece; also the range of sounds from low to high in which the singer is at ease
Triste	sad
Tutto or tutti	all sing, as in a finale
Vellutati	velvety
Verismo	a style of dramatic opera developed after the earlier (late nineteenth century) operas of Rossini, Donizetti, and Bellini
Voce	voice
Vivace	lively

The Singer's Library: Suggested Readings

Ardoin, John, *Callas at Juilliard*. New York: Alfred, A. Knopf, 1987.

Blivet, Jean-Pierre, *La Voie du Chant*, Paris: Librairie Arthème Fayard, 1999.

Caesari, Herbert, *The Voice of the Mind*, London: Robert Hale, Ltd, 1951.

Cameron, Julia, *The Artist's Way*, New York: H.P. Putnam & Sons, 1992 (paperback).

Celletti, Rodolfo, *Il Canto*, Garzanti Italia, 1989.

Chekhov, Michael, *To The Actor*. New York: Harper Bros., 1953.

Clark, Mark Ross, *Singing, Acting and Movement in Opera*. Bloomington, IN: Indiana Univ. Press, 2002.

Douglas, Nigel, *Legendary Voices*. London: Andre Deutsch Ltd., 1992.

Drake, James A, *Rosa Ponselle: A Centenary Biography*. Pompton Plains, NJ: Amadeus Press, 1997.

Gelb, Michael J., *How To Think Like Leonardo da Vinci*. New York: Dell Publishing, 1998.

Glass, Beaumont, *Lotte Lehmann: A Life in Opera & Song*. Santa Barbara: Capra Press, 1988 (Note: I am mentioned on p.252).

Green, Barry, with Timothy Gallwey, *The Inner Game of Music*. New York: Doubleday, 1986.

Hahn, Reynaldo, *On Singers and Singing*. Pompton Plains, NJ: Amadeus Press, 1990.

Huang, Al, and Jerry Lynch, *Thinking Body, Dancing Mind*. New York: Bantam Books, 1994 (paperback).

Le Gallienne, Eva, *The Mystic in the Theater: Eleonora Duse*. New York: Farrar, Straus and Geroux, 1966 (reprinted in paperback).

Lehmann, Lotte, *More Than Singing*. London: Boosey & Hawkes, Inc., 1945 (exists in paperback).

Ristad, Eloise, *A Soprano on Her Head*. Moab, UT: Real People Press, 1982 (paperback).

Rosselli, John, *Singers of Italian Opera*. London: Cambridge Univ. Press, 1992.

Steane, J. B., *Singers of the Century*. Pompton Plains, NJ: Amadeus Press, 1996.

Index of Singers, Conductors and Teachers

Contents of Accompanying CD